TH
IS

A STEP-BY-STEP WORKBOOK

WHAT

for Identifying Your Values, Priorities,

MATTERS

and Path Forward after a Crisis

DR. PERPETUA NEO

ADAMS MEDIA

NEW YORK   LONDON   TORONTO   SYDNEY   NEW DELHI

Adams Media
An Imprint of Simon & Schuster, Inc.
100 Technology Center Drive
Stoughton, Massachusetts 02072

Copyright © 2022 by Simon & Schuster, Inc.

First Adams Media trade paperback edition May 2022

ADAMS MEDIA and colophon are trademarks of Simon & Schuster.

For information about special discounts for bulk purchases, please contact Simon &
Schuster Special Sales at 1-866-506-1949 or business@simonandschuster.com.

The Simon & Schuster Speakers Bureau can bring authors to your live event. For more
information or to book an event contact the Simon & Schuster Speakers Bureau at
1-866-248-3049 or visit our website at www.simonspeakers.com.

Interior design by Julia Jacintho

Manufactured in the United States of America

1 2022

ISBN 978-1-5072-1852-5
ISBN 978-1-5072-1853-2 (ebook)

DEDICATION

To my parents and grandparents,
for teaching me that I have nine lives,
each brighter and wiser than the last.

CONTENTS

INTRODUCTION

If you're reading this, something in your life has changed. It could be a sudden illness that has you questioning everything you had assumed about the future. Maybe it's a loss of some kind, such as the passing of a loved one, that has left you feeling stuck. Or it could be something that you thought would be positive, like a promotion, that has caused unexpected anxiety.

Regardless of the situation, what matters is that you're going through it—*it's real for you*. And while it may be difficult to see it this way now, this experience offers a unique opportunity: It's a chance to look at your life with fresh eyes and reevaluate what is important. Is what you're doing in line with your larger goals? Do your daily habits and priorities reflect the things you deeply value?

If your answer to these questions is no, that's okay. *This Is What Matters* is here to help you get back on track with what is truly important and let go of what isn't. In Chapter 1, you'll learn how to not just accept but partner with the reality of what's happening in your life in order to make beneficial changes. You'll also reflect honestly on what the journey from crisis to living a life aligned to what matters will look like, and how to stay motivated and optimistic through the highs and lows of your progress.

Then, you'll use fifty guided exercises to reflect across the main areas of your life, from your relationships and home to your career and personal values. In each chapter, you'll consider what you'd like more of and less of in one of these areas, and what you can do about this right now. You'll set specific intentions and goals for the chapter, learn why each exercise matters, explore what you've learned as a result, and discover a plan to take action using the insights you've gained.

Building your new life around what matters consists of building new habits, and the exercises in this book will guide you in deciding the habits that are needed for creating a life that is meaningful to *you*. Of course, like building muscles in the gym, these habits can feel difficult to keep up at first. At the end of every chapter, you'll engage in a series of rituals to maximize your success.

You'll:

- Reward yourself.
- Get clear on what stands in the way.
- Schedule regular check-ins.

As you work through this book, you'll see that nestled within this crisis is the opportunity to design the life you want going forward. Time will pass no matter what you do: Let's make it pay dividends for you. Here's to a good life that you've designed, *thoughtfully*.

CHAPTER 1

Accepting *What Is* So You Can Discover *What Matters*

When you think about the people in your life who've been through some sort of crisis, you'll realize that everyone is changed by experiencing difficult circumstances. Consider the folktale about the girl who saw life as a miserable series of never-ending problems: Her father put a potato, an egg, and coffee beans into three pots of boiling water, inviting her to reflect on how each was changed by the water. The potato grew soft and weak, the egg became hard inside, and the coffee beans turned the water into something aromatic and delicious. In the boiling water that is crisis, people can allow themselves to crumble under the weight of what has happened, become hardened and bitter about it, or turn that difficulty into a chance to adapt and thrive. The question here is, what will *you* choose to do?

Crisis is an invitation to reflect on your life and who you are—and what you *want* life to be and who you *want* to become. In the midst of whatever the world has thrown at you is a prime opportunity to take stock of what truly matters to you, and whether your current goals and habits are aligned with those values. Maybe you've forgotten your old dreams, or traded parts of yourself that you felt pressured to change. In this chapter, you'll explore more about how crisis can be used to remember who you are—your values, dreams, strengths, and experiences so far—and decide what you'd like to fill the rest of your life with.

HOW TO ACCEPT REALITY

The first step in the journey of discovering what matters is to accept reality, which understandably asks a lot of you. The truth is, people are wired to cope with reality by self-soothing. This often means choosing actions that make you feel temporarily good or numb, but come with a heavy emotional and physical hangover that increases your dependence on these Band-Aid solutions. On a deeper level, what's really happening is that you are building more pathways in your brain, body, and behaviors that keep you stuck in helplessness and hurt after a crisis.

You can counteract these ineffective coping mechanisms by making the decision to partner with reality. This means accepting what's going on for you right now as a *fact of the present moment*. For instance, your shoulders may be feeling heavy, and you feel terrified. Acknowledging these feelings means you reclaim your power. Throughout this book, you'll find exercises that help you accept and gain perspective on what is happening and how you are feeling. Completing these exercises will give you a clearer mind, and then you can strategize and take action toward how you'd like to solve the issue at hand, allowing you to journey closer to your best self.

WHAT TO EXPECT ON THIS JOURNEY

Before you can explore what matters and make a plan for bringing those things into your life, it's important to be aware of what you will likely encounter along the way. This includes the initial feelings as you deal with a crisis, and how it will feel as you shift onto the path of healing and future happiness offered by the exercises in this book. You've experienced something pivotal, and it's going to have an effect on you.

The human brain is built to believe that good things will happen to you, the world is a nice place, and the future is bright. But when crisis strikes, your world of assumptions shatters. Suddenly your brain believes the opposite: *Bad things will happen. The world is a dangerous place. The future is bad.* Because, after all, you've gone through it. It is in your brain's interest to watch out for any danger, to protect you. And sometimes, you will see benign things as threats, and interact with the world in a way that only fulfills your worst nightmares.

When dealing with a crisis, you will also romanticize the past: Everything was rosier "back then." You forget the parts of yourself that weren't helpful and the things that happened that weren't so wonderful. Instead, you'll focus on and likely exaggerate what was good before this difficult time.

You'll feel heartbreak, loss, grief, anger, relief—a confusing cocktail that causes the primitive parts of your brain to hijack the wise, strategic parts of your brain, switching you to autopilot. Here, the brain goes into threat mode, that automatic response that evolved to keep humans alive, and it becomes difficult for you to make intentional, well-thought-out decisions. You may find yourself automatically grabbing hold of any tactic that someone suggests or that you've read about—anything to feel better or feel like you're solving the problem as quickly as possible. But when a course of action is rushed without looking at the bigger picture such as what will happen over time to yourself, your relationships, your work, etc., you are likely to just create more messes to clean up in the future.

In the chapters that follow, you'll be flipping the switch from autopilot to manual mode—making the intentional choice to override biology that's concerned only with basic survival. In choosing to take control, you will shift gears to heal, fortify the parts of you that made you vulnerable, and live the future you deserve. And with every step that you take from this point forward, you will grow your hope and strength. You will rebuild that bridge between the past and your future that crisis shattered. In the process, you will make meaning of the past and of what you're going through now. You will discover and appreciate the resources inside and outside of you that you can leverage. You will feel lighter because you've released things you picked up along your life's path that weren't quite you or that you've outgrown.

And so, choosing to grow through a crisis is how you create a sense of coherence between what happened then and what will happen in the future. You'll be able to say, "I used this chapter to become someone I'm proud of, and to wholeheartedly live."

Although there are certain things you can anticipate along the way, this journey from present challenges to a future aligned with what matters isn't the same from person to person. Everyone's journey is unique, and there will be ups and downs that differ from what you may see in someone else's experiences. Remember this, especially when you're tempted to compare. After all, the things that matter to someone else might matter to you differently. During these times, don't pay attention to the critical voices in your head or any naysayers around you; strong, tactful boundaries will protect you from thoughts and opinions that only serve to make you feel worse.

Focus on the good things and your progress, even though your brain will naturally focus on what's not done *yet*. And when things are not going well—for reasons ranging from mood to being new to this to taking a chance—view this as data you can learn from and use to improve your efforts. Instead of giving up, discard whatever is not serving you well and move on. Every day that you show up for yourself, you become the champion your younger self never had. And every time that you choose to commit to recommitting, you're taking another successful step forward. Choose to see the big picture of how your small steps are leading to a happier, more authentic life. Choose to keep practicing being your best future self. Because things don't get better by chance, but by thoughtful change.

Be sure to take good care of your physical body throughout these changes as well, so it can support your healing and growth. This includes the fundamentals of eating nutritious food, drinking sufficient water, and sleeping adequately. You might also want to use magnesium and vitamin B supplements to support your nervous system and energy levels; talk to your doctor about this option. Also, make sure you commit to moving even just a little bit every day—whether it's a short walk after breakfast or a longer run, staying active does wonders to enhance your health and well-being.

How to Tap In to Hope

As you journey through crisis and cultivate the things that matter to you, hope will be invaluable. You are born with hope—it's what fuels you through your darkest moments and gives you that extra boost when things are going great. Always nurture your sense of hope. Maybe that means remembering all the times you've pulled through (or having someone else remind you of those times). Or maybe it means using prayer or looking to something bigger than yourself, such as a faith-based practice or spiritual circle. Sometimes it's simply trusting that you will reap the harvest of the work you are doing now, even if you can't yet see exactly what the outcome might be. In good times and bad, keep your hope stores full. Most importantly, know that you are *never* alone.

TURNING THE PAGE TO DISCOVER WHAT MATTERS

Now that you know more about what to expect and how to navigate the highs and lows of healing and growing from crisis, it's time to determine just what matters to you and start taking steps to get it. In the next pages of this book, you'll reevaluate the things you prioritize, get rid of what stands in the way, and develop the mindsets and skills to support the changes you make.

Before getting into the exercises in each chapter, you'll first identify intentions and set goals related to the insights explored in that chapter. An intention is how you want to feel, or who you want to be, as a result of going on this journey. A goal is something you want to accomplish. Knowing why you are doing something helps you commit, and pinpointing what you want from a certain area of your life helps you map the way forward (and notice if you start to lose focus and get distracted away from your goal).

Each chapter ends with a plan to further help you achieve success by prompting you to:

- Reward yourself for the progress made. Rewards maximize success because you consistently feel good about what you do, which makes you want to keep doing it over and over again, turning your new actions into a discipline.

- **Figure out what stands in the way.** The human brain doesn't like change, which can make progressing toward your goals difficult. Getting clear on what obstacles might come up will help you be aware of potential stumbling blocks. And when you're at risk of being thrown off course, you know how to respond and move forward.

- **Check in on your progress.** When you start establishing a new habit, you may second-guess yourself at times. This steals mental energy. When you have check-ins scheduled in, you bypass that doubt, knowing that you can simply refine the process during your reviews. Check-ins also let you notice sooner rather than later if you start to lose focus on your goals.

The future you want is waiting for you. It's up to you to take control and claim what matters most!

CHAPTER 2

Discovering What Matters to You

Getting to know yourself is one of the most valuable journeys you can ever take in life. Sometimes you trick yourself about what's going on or about what you want. That can end up making you feel more lost. And then, there are so many ideas buzzing about what to do next—you wonder which is the right course.

The truth is, it's a matter of discerning what's right for *you*. Meaning, you have to know who you are, fundamentally. In this chapter, you'll reflect on who you are, what your life is like right now, and what you want out of life. You'll also learn more about your patterns of behaviors and beliefs, so you will know your headspace better. This way, you build solid foundations within yourself. Based on these foundations, you'll craft a plan to put yourself in a place of calmness and control, so you can face the different emotions in your life—the good, bad, and neutral—and make decisions grounded in wisdom. You are the foundation of everything you do. It all starts with mastering yourself.

SETTING INTENTIONS AND GOALS

To support your success in the exercises that follow, answer these questions about your intentions and goals for this chapter.

I want to feel _____ about myself.

As I discover what matters to me, I want to become the type of person who _____

_____.

This is what I want to accomplish from discovering what matters to me:	These are the mini-milestones I'm breaking this larger goal into:

EXAMINE YOUR LIFE IN FIVE QUESTIONS

Before you can make a change—or even determine whether you want or need a change—you have to take stock of what is. What does your life look and feel like right now? What do *you* look like right now—to yourself and to the people around you? How do you feel about yourself? And what can you be grateful for?

The following "five questions" exercise will help you determine what's going in the right direction, and what could be different about yourself and your life.

1. Do you like who you see?

This question is about the person you see in the mirror or in photos. How you feel inside impacts the way you look. For instance, if you're not feeling at peace with your life, your smile may look forced in photos.

What's going right: What could be different:

_____   _____

_____   _____

_____   _____

_____   _____

_____   _____

2. Do you like your life?

This question is about your everyday life as well as your breaks (weekends, time out from your usual routine, holidays). Consider the different areas of your life, how you live, and the roles you play. For most people, their jobs, resources, relationships, and energy levels heavily influence their answer to this question.

What's going right: What could be different:

_____   _____

_____   _____

_____   _____

_____   _____

_____   _____

3. Do you like who you are?

How you see yourself as a person revolves around your personality, the choices you make, and the values by which you live your life.

What's going right:

_____

_____

_____

_____

_____

What could be different:

_____

_____

_____

_____

_____

4. Do you own your past?

Pain and negative experiences are inevitable. But some people find it hard to acknowledge these chapters of their life. Others hesitate to acknowledge their role in creating positive outcomes, instead writing them off as luck. Think about your life's journey so far—what can you acknowledge?

What's going right:

_____

_____

_____

_____

_____

What could be different:

_____

_____

_____

_____

_____

5. **Do you like who you're becoming?**

Every choice you make now, and every action you take, is shaping your future. For example, if you typically eat healthy foods and sleep enough at night, you are more likely to have better physical health than the people who usually turn to fast food for their meals and get just a few hours of sleep every night. The same holds for what you do and don't do in your day-to-day life, whether in your job or relationships, or to build your mental muscles. Consider the person you are growing into, based on what you do now.

What's going right:

_____

_____

_____

_____

What could be different:

_____

_____

_____

_____

Understanding Why This Matters

People sometimes dismiss the entirety of their lives and who they are, especially during a crisis, because their brains zero in on only the negative aspects and the losses. At other times, they may be unrealistically positive, taking for granted that all is good and ignoring what could benefit from a change. This exercise provides you with clarity about the parts you accept and like—about your life and who you are—and which parts you'd like to change. This builds a sense of gratitude for yourself and what you've done right, and for others and how they may have helped pave your way.

And because the exercise looks at the past, present, *and* future, you are able to create a story about who you are, what makes you who you are, and who you might become. This understanding helps you to gain a sense of closure about what happened in the past and control over what will happen in the future—keys to growing from a crisis.

Connecting with What Matters

Use the following questions to reflect on what you've identified from this exercise.

Here's what I've realized
about myself:

_____

_____

_____

_____

_____

_____

_____

_____

_____

_____

_____

_____

_____

_____

_____

_____

This is the one
thing I'm most grateful for:

_____

_____

_____

_____

_____

_____

_____

This is the one thing that
urgently needs to change:

_____

_____

_____

_____

_____

_____

_____

Taking Action on What Matters

Now it's time to make the changes you've identified in this exercise! For each of the five questions, you will identify the mindsets, habits, and constraints that stand in the way of being able to answer the questions with a "yes." Then you will begin to craft an action plan for overcoming these obstacles and making those changes. (This plan may include the help of a partner or a professional.)

1. Do you like who you see?

Changes to make:	What's in the way?	First steps to make:
_____	_____	_____
_____	_____	_____
_____	_____	_____
_____	_____	_____
_____	_____	_____
_____	_____	_____

2. Do you like your life?

Changes to make:	What's in the way?	First steps to make:
_____	_____	_____
_____	_____	_____
_____	_____	_____
_____	_____	_____
_____	_____	_____
_____	_____	_____
_____	_____	_____

3. Do you like who you are?

Changes to make:	What's in the way?	First steps to make:

4. Do you own your past?

Changes to make:	What's in the way?	First steps to make:

5. Do you like who you're becoming?

Changes to make:	What's in the way?	First steps to make:

DESIGN YOUR GOOD LIFE

What makes a life "good" is different for everyone. Generally, this means a happy life or a purposeful life, or, as researchers Lorraine Besser and Shigehiro Oishi found, a psychologically rich life. Any combination or version of these focuses can make life feel good—you don't need to choose just one. You can design your own Good Life that focuses on what matters to you. In this exercise, you'll reflect on the parts of each of the elements of the Good Life that resonate with you:

- *A happy life* includes positive emotions, stability, and comfort. It involves some degree of good luck, like having the resources to live a satisfactory life while avoiding major conflicts or disasters.
- *A purposeful life* is about living with meaning and service. People who live purposeful lives may be guided by specific values, morals, spirituality, or religion; pursue growth; or contribute to a larger cause or community.
- *A psychologically rich life* is one where the aesthetic of living, from finding beauty in everyday things to exploring the depths of inner experience, is emphasized. This life is suited to any budget—as long as you are open and curious!—and people living psychologically rich lives often have a treasure trove of exciting stories to tell.

Understanding Why This Matters

It's easy to give the responsibility to your culture or your community to tell you what a Good Life is, but ultimately it's you who has to define your best life. Until you can articulate what you truly want, you will feel dissatisfied—no matter how much you achieve. Breaking things down into the three categories of happiness, meaning, and psychological richness will help you to consider what you already have, and what you want more of.

Connecting with What Matters

Learning about the different types of the Good Life, here's what I've reflected about my own life:

_____

_____

_____

_____

_____

_____

_____

_____

_____

_____

_____

_____

_____

_____

_____

_____

_____

_____

_____

Here's how I felt about myself:

_____

_____

_____

_____

_____

_____

_____

_____

_____

_____

Here's what I want more or less of:

_____

_____

_____

_____

_____

_____

_____

_____

_____

Taking Action on What Matters

Here are some prompts to help you explore how you can amp up each of the three elements in your own Good Life. Use the space provided to reflect.

Happiness:

What makes you joyful or delighted? What would you need more of, in order to feel more content?

_____

_____

_____

_____

Meaning:

What do you need to do to grow personally and/or professionally? How can you make sense of your past, present, and future? What causes or communities can you devote some of your energy to?

_____

_____

_____

_____

Psychological richness:

What can you fill your life with that will make your experiences more interesting or beautiful? Are there specific practices that might enable you to better access your inner life?

_____

_____

_____

_____

_____

IDENTIFY YOUR COGNITIVE PHOTOSHOP FILTERS

When people experience an uncomfortable situation, they often suppress the associated feelings by using logic, gratitude, or extra positivity. I call this response "Cognitive Photoshop" because it involves turning on certain "filters" through which you want to see a situation. And while these tools may be helpful when life is generally stable, they fall short at other times, especially during a crisis or when things feel overwhelming. This is because you know you are lying to yourself. And so, the space between perception and reality widens. With time, this causes a deep internal conflict because a part of you knows that reality is difficult, but another part of you insists that it isn't—you are essentially gaslighting yourself. Not acknowledging your experiences diminishes your personal sense of control, and the resulting helplessness you feel means your confidence in handling your own head-space gets smaller and smaller.

The following are examples of Cognitive Photoshop filters. Think of these like the filters you may be familiar with on photo editing or social media apps. Rank them from 1-8 according to which ones you are most likely to use, 1 being the least likely and 8 being the most likely.

_____Contrast: You convince yourself you're supposed to deny how you're feeling because someone else has got it worse, using statements like "It's no big deal, other people are suffering far more."

_____Brightness: You use phrases like "Think positive!" and "Be proactive!" to bypass the parts of your situation that aren't so "bright" or secure.

_____Highlights: You doggedly find reasons to be grateful, turning to hollow phrases that don't mean much to you, like "Blue skies" or "I have a job," only to feel worse because you are just finding any random thing that doesn't have true value to you.

- ___Empathy:___ You may say things like "Hurt people hurt people" to justify letting others get away with recurring bad behavior; you have more empathy for others than you do for yourself.

- ___Stuff Happens:___ Just because deaths, losses, and dilemmas are inevitable, you expect yourself to suck it up and keep moving forward without grieving or processing. So you say things like "That's part of life; I'm okay"...when you're not really okay.

- ___Special Snowflake:___ You think you're the only one going through this difficult experience, or you think that everyone else who has experienced it dealt with it better. Therefore, you judge yourself as weak or "too" emotional.

- ___Quick Fix:___ You tell yourself that a temporary crutch, like a drink or exercise, will miraculously solve the problem. These temporary Band-Aids don't address the root cause and may just make you feel worse over time.

- ___Time Travel:___ When you feel haunted by the past, you scold yourself, "It was so long ago!" and you should just "snap out of it!" or "get over it." Except that a part of you hasn't quite processed the past yet.

Understanding Why This Matters

Applying Cognitive Photoshop to tough feelings or situations is one of the fastest ways to feel like you're not in control of your mind, and to build up a sense of helplessness over time. Even if Cognitive Photoshop works sometimes, you can't simply think your way to a happier or more positive or "rational" emotional state without getting to the bottom of what is happening and why you are feeling the way you are. This is because suppressing your feelings causes them to build up in your body, and they will eventually erupt with a vengeance. You can see this in the form of physical illnesses, burnout, or panic attacks; it's a high price to pay, especially because you may experience it multiple times throughout your life.

These are the Cognitive Photoshop filters I should be aware of that I am likely to use:

_____

_____

_____

_____

_____

_____

_____

These are the types of situations where I'm most likely to use these filters:

_____

_____

_____

_____

_____

_____

_____

Taking Action on What Matters

Seeing your feelings and thoughts for what they are and owning your right to them leads to knowing what you really want in life. Now that you've identified the Cognitive Photoshop filters you are likely to use (and may already be using), be aware every time they pop up.

1. When you find yourself using a filter, pause. Use the guide in the Assign Colors to Your Emotions exercise later in this chapter to acknowledge your experiences honestly and then reset your brain with three deep breaths. Then do something that helps you clear your mind and reach a place of clarity, so you can tackle the root issue head-on. Maybe it's taking a walk, talking to someone you trust, or a quick power nap.

2. Commit to this exercise every time an uncomfortable thought or feeling pops up; with time, you'll find it easier to reach that place of calmness from which it's easier to determine the best action going forward.

RESET YOUR BRAIN

The amygdala, or fear center, in your brain kicks in whenever it detects a threat. This mechanism evolved in animals so they can react quickly. Even if you think you're not that stressed, or can convince yourself otherwise, the amygdala hijacks at least part of your higher brain. What's your higher brain exactly? It's the part of you that makes you human: It allows you to strategize, organize, and delay gratification. Therefore, it is important to keep resetting your brain whenever you feel stressed, so you consistently make wiser decisions instead of jumping straight to that fear response. With a clear head, you figure out and focus on what matters to you, and also decide what to do when those pesky stressors pop up to try to thwart your progress.

This exercise teaches you to reset your brain quickly, without needing to meditate for hours a day. It also helps you to process and release whatever you're dealing with. After this exercise, the following Assign Colors to Your Emotions exercise will show you how to get even more clarity.

To reset your brain after encountering a stressful situation, complete these steps:

1. Acknowledge the situation without judging it, with the same neutrality with which you accept the fact that the sky is blue.
2. Ground yourself by shuffling your feet on the floor slowly.
3. Take a deep breath in through your nose, making sure you're inflating your belly like a balloon, then exhale completely out through your nose, making sure you're deflating your belly. As you breathe out, allow your shoulders to drop and visualize releasing everything that makes you tense. Repeat two more times.
4. Notice how you feel and acknowledge the calmness and clarity that's taken the place of tension.
5. Tell yourself, "Thank you for showing up for me," with as much gratitude as you can tap in to.

Understanding Why This Matters

When you judge yourself, you compound the threat your amygdala detects because it goes into an even deeper level of fear mode. Through that negative lens, you see any threat or stressor as *more* of a threat or stressor than it really is. Acknowledging your experiences objectively sets a neutral tone that keeps the stress you already feel from building up. Shuffling your feet brings you back into your body and away from your busy mind. Deep breathing calms your amygdala, switching on your vagus nerve (which is in charge of calming your nervous system), and relaxing your body. Thanking yourself means you acknowledge what you've done to help yourself through this stressful experience. The dopamine that floods your brain as you thank yourself will make you want to repeat this exercise, creating a habit every time you take a deep breath.

Connecting with What Matters

This is how I felt as I did the brain reset exercise:

_____

_____

_____

_____

_____

_____

_____

_____

_____

The easiest part of the exercise was:

_____

_____

_____

_____

The most difficult part of the exercise was:

_____

_____

_____

_____

Practice this exercise first thing in the morning and right before you go to sleep. This way, it becomes second nature by the time you're really in need of a reset. Another opportunity for practice is as you transition from one task to another. You can visualize this act as clearing the energetic debris of the previous task, so you enter the next task with a clean slate.

You can also pair your breathing with an essential oil to help the activity, because smells shortcut to the primitive parts of your brain where the fear response gets triggered. Try energizing eucalyptus or peppermint earlier in the day, and calming lavender at night.

ASSIGN COLORS TO YOUR EMOTIONS

To truly discover and honor what matters to you, you must first recognize what's going on in your head and body right now. You will practice this exercise in three types of circumstances: when you're feeling good, when you're feeling neutral, and when you're feeling bad. You can also imagine yourself back in a situation you already experienced, recalling as vividly as possible the sights, sounds, tastes, and sensations of that time.

Give yourself privacy and time to reflect, so you can connect deeply with what's going on (or imagine that previous situation). Answer these questions as honestly as you can. Say what you really feel (or felt), not what you wish you felt or think you should feel. If you have more than one emotion or sensation, write those down too.

A situation where you feel good:

Here's what's going on for me now:

_____

_____

Here's how I am feeling in this situation:

_____

_____

Here's the context of the situation that I'm facing right now:

_____

_____

I experience this feeling in this part of my body:

_____

_____

These are the main thoughts going through my head:

_____

_____

If I were to intuitively give this feeling a color, it would be:

_____

_____

A situation where you feel neutral:

Here's what's going on for
me now:

_____

_____

Here's how I am feeling
in this situation:

_____

_____

Here's the context of the situation
that I'm facing right now:

_____

_____

I experience this feeling in this
part of my body:

_____

_____

These are the main thoughts
going through my head:

_____

_____

If I were to intuitively give this
feeling a color, it would be:

_____

_____

A situation where you feel bad:

Here's what's going on for
me now:

_____

_____

Here's how I am feeling
in this situation:

_____

_____

Here's the context of the situation
that I'm facing right now:

_____

_____

I experience this feeling in this
part of my body:

_____

_____

These are the main thoughts
going through my head:

_____

_____

If I were to intuitively give this
feeling a color, it would be:

_____

_____

Understanding Why This Matters

Often, we downplay or suppress our experiences. You may force yourself to feel positive, grateful, or logical when really you're feeling anxious or frustrated (see the earlier Identify Your Cognitive Photoshop Filters exercise for more about this). People do this because they are scared to acknowledge what's going on and feel powerless and uncomfortable (and no one wants to feel this way). But the reality is that acknowledging what's going on means you regain power over the situation.

Distinguishing between your feelings, thoughts, and body sensations gives you clarity. Specifically, when you tease out your main thoughts, looking at them objectively as colors and data, you can focus on whether the thoughts are connected to a belief that is relevant and/or helpful or one that is irrelevant and/or unhelpful. Sometimes, you might only be able to name what you're feeling; other times, you can only identify the thoughts or body sensations. That's okay. With practice, you'll develop a more sophisticated vocabulary as you become more in tune with yourself.

From this clarity, you can create an action plan to move forward accordingly, either letting go of what is irrelevant and/or unhelpful or putting to use what *is* relevant and/or helpful as you pursue what matters.

Connecting with What Matters

Here's how acknowledging my feelings and assigning those feelings as colors feels:

_____

_____

_____

_____

_____

Here's what I've learned about the connection between my thoughts, feelings, and what goes on in my body:

_____

_____

_____

_____

_____

On a scale of 1–5, rank the following in order of what is the easiest to identify, 1 being the least easy and 5 being the easiest.

_____The main situation

_____My thoughts

_____My feelings

_____The location(s) I feel these
things in my body

_____The color of my feelings

Based on my rankings, these
are what I need more practice
in identifying:

_____

_____

_____

_____

Here's how each aspect of your reflection helps you gain the clarity
needed to move forward:

- Situation: This helps you to focus on the main crux of the situation,
  instead of being distracted by outside concerns.
- Thoughts: Knowing your thoughts, you can ask, "What does this
  thought tell me about the situation/myself/the future?" and "Is this
  thought true/relevant/helpful?"
- Feelings: Naming your feelings lets you know if how you're feeling is complex (having multiple and/or conflicting emotions) or simple (having one
  main emotion). When your feelings are simple, it can be easier to move
  forward. But when your feelings are complex, they stop you from moving
  forward because you experience them as a big, overwhelming mass—or feel
  bad for having mixed emotions. You must address these feelings of over-
  whelm and/or shame before getting into the root emotions themselves.
- Body sensations: Knowing where feelings make themselves known
  in your body, you can ask, "How can I take better care of this body
  part?" when this feeling comes up again. For instance, if you store
  anxiety in your neck, rub your neck gently or get a massage.
- Color: By seeing your feeling as a color, you teach your brain that this
  feeling is a temporary piece of information; it doesn't have to last forever.

KNOW HOW YOU ESCAPE

It's natural to worry when you are facing a crisis. But worry zaps your mental fitness and significantly compromises your energy. So sometimes, people turn to certain activities to escape and self-soothe. However, escapism isn't always helpful. This exercise will help you identify your escapes and their triggers, as well as whether these are helpful. From there, you can thoughtfully decide if you want to continue with these behaviors.

Escapism can take many forms, including:

- Something that *seems* productive (e.g., worrying, trying to solve others' problems when not asked to)
- Something fun or rewarding (e.g., drinking, binge-watching)
- Something consciously self-destructive (e.g., using substances)

The crux is that the unhealthy or unhelpful behavior provides *temporary* relief, costs you energy and well-being, and is something you'll regret. You might engage in these behaviors both to avoid worry and *after* you've indulged in overthinking. Identify how you escape by answering the following questions.

This is what I do to escape my own head:

_____

_____

_____

_____

_____

_____

_____

_____

These are the things that trigger escape for me:

_____

_____

_____

_____

_____

_____

_____

_____

Here are the excuses I make to justify this behavior:

_____

_____

_____

_____

_____

Here's how I feel after an escape:

_____

_____

_____

_____

_____

When I engage in any of these behaviors from a *healthy* place, here's how I feel:

_____

_____

_____

_____

Understanding Why This Matters

Reflecting on the escapism cycle helps you break the cycle and figure out what you can do differently going forward. So, you regain self-control.

You also get clear about the complexity behind certain actions. Some things can be both reward and punishment. For example, a single glass of champagne after meeting a big goal and drinking yourself into a stupor are both drinking, but each has different consequences. This exercise teaches you to get honest with yourself, so you choose to avoid escape behaviors and focus on those that will get you to what matters in your life.

These are the escape behaviors
I'll look out for:

Here's what I'll do differently,
instead of indulging in an
unhealthy or unhelpful escape:

_____

_____

_____

_____

_____

_____

_____

_____

_____

Taking Action on What Matters

Before or after worrying and overthinking, try the breathing activity in the Reset Your Brain exercise earlier in this chapter. This brings the wiser, strategic parts of your brain back online, so you make decisions from more intentional space. You avoid tumbling down that rabbit hole of escape behaviors.

Also remember that you won't shake off these escape behaviors instantly; they didn't develop overnight, and they've given you relief in the past, no matter how temporary. As you work through them, take note of the things that help you successfully overcome them.

PURSUE ORDER, JOY, AND MASTERY

This next exercise shows you how to positively channel your energy. Instead of regretting how you spend your time, you can use it in ways that pay dividends for your present and future. Some enriching ways to spend time are in the pursuit of *order*, *joy*, or *mastery*. This exercise explains these different pursuits and helps you identify specific ways you can actively work toward each.

1. Order

Order refers to things that create a sense of orderliness in your life. Often, a lack of orderliness in your surroundings can reflect disorder in your mind, so getting organized with your external life can help you create more internal order, leaving space and energy to focus on what matters. Creating order could be *physical*, relating to the objects around you, or *digital*, such as computer folders.

These are the things that
need cleaning:

_____

_____

_____

_____

_____

_____

_____

_____

_____

_____

These are the things that
need organizing:

_____

_____

_____

_____

_____

_____

_____

_____

_____

_____

2. Joy

Joy refers to things that matter to your sense of happiness or contentment. Joy can result from an experience (like savoring your favorite food), or from pausing to feel content with what you have (like the people surrounding you or your cozy home), or from something that emotionally moves you (like observing a beautiful sunset or hugging your pet).

These are the things that create joy in my life:

_____

_____

_____

_____

_____

3. Mastery

Mastery refers to the personal or professional skills that you start or continue, without being perfect at them. Perhaps it's something you've always wanted to learn, like a language or a craft, or something you stopped doing and want to continue again.

Here's what I'd love to start: Here's what I'd love to continue:

_____   _____

_____   _____

_____   _____

_____   _____

_____   _____

_____   _____

_____   _____

_____   _____

Understanding Why This Matters

In a crisis, it's common to feel tired or sorry for yourself and use this as an excuse to worry or escape. Having an order/joy/mastery list to refer to means you no longer have an excuse to default to. Even if it feels hard at first, you can pick the simplest thing on the list. This creates momentum to help you feel more in control of your day and your internal climate.

Connecting with What Matters

Using the lists I made previously, here are the simplest things I can do when the days feel toughest:

_____

_____

_____

_____

_____

_____

Here are the things I'll enjoy the most:

_____

_____

_____

_____

_____

Taking Action on What Matters

Whenever you feel overwhelmed or compelled to overthink, pick something to do on your list. As you engage with the tasks, take pauses to acknowledge that you've shown up for yourself, and note what you've accomplished. Also, reward yourself for doing these things! As you learned in Chapter 1, rewards spark a release of feel-good chemicals in your brain that inspire you to keep up with your list instead of defaulting to overthinking.

KNOW HOW YOU RECHARGE, REPLENISH, AND REJUVENATE

Sometimes, despite the best of intentions, you may think *I don't know what to do*, whether it's what to do to feel in control, or what to do with your day. Or you don't know how to take care of yourself. The problem is that because we never learned about self-care at school, we follow what's prescribed on social media, what we see other people doing, and generic advice online. That's great if you happen to enjoy those things, but if you don't, you wonder why you feel worse after. The truth is, you already have the answers.

This "three Rs" exercise is designed to help you figure out the self-care that works for you by zeroing in on how you best *recharge*, *replenish*, and *rejuvenate*. For each of the prompts, think back on previous activities that have allowed you to achieve these states. They could be active pursuits, like running or journaling, or passive ones, like napping or sipping some tea. Being able to take care of yourself means feeling more in control of your mind and energy, even if you're going through a challenging time. It also means you can short-circuit any vicious cycles that people often find themselves in when the going gets tough. (Plus, you deserve special care, no matter what you are or aren't going through.)

Imagine if you were a phone and the battery was running low. What would you need to do to fill up that battery again quickly?

This is how you *recharge* yourself:

_____

_____

_____

_____

Now think back to a time when you woke up feeling completely refreshed and ready to take on the day, as though your battery was 100 percent full. What activities do you do in order to feel this way?

This is how you *replenish* yourself:

_____

_____

_____

_____

Then recall a time when you felt brand-new within, like your cells had completely renewed. More importantly, you were brimming with inspiration. It was as though your battery wasn't just full; you had a spare battery pack too. What things did you do to feel that way?

This is how you *rejuvenate* yourself:

_____

_____

_____

_____

Understanding Why This Matters

You are you and you do you. A person who's type A might rejuvenate by running and recharge with timed puzzles. A beauty-loving type B might replenish by stretching on the yoga mat, and recharge with a cup of mindfully brewed tea. It all depends on what feels best to you.

The "three Rs" exercise gives you a concrete list of your salves, nourishments, and renewers. These activities heal you during difficult times and gift you with an extra boost during good times.

Connecting with What Matters

These are the activities I've previously enjoyed but have lost touch with:

_____

_____

_____

_____

_____

_____

_____

Here's what doing this exercise felt like:

_____

_____

_____

_____

_____

_____

_____

Taking Action on What Matters

1. Set a photo of your "three Rs" list as the wallpaper on your phone or computer. This way, you'll have quick access to it.
2. Schedule your "three Rs" activities in your weekly calendar and commit to them.
3. Reward yourself when you've done any of these activities.
4. If you forget an appointment to recharge, replenish, or rejuvenate, that's okay. We all forget sometimes. What matters most is to have the mindset that you'll always commit to recommitting.

HARNESS SURVIVOR'S GUILT FOR GOOD

Going through a crisis is always communal in some sense, even if you sometimes feel alone in the process. On the more obvious end, it could be a collective crisis like a pandemic or war. Then there are the more personal struggles you face that others also have been through before. And because you may seem to be weathering the storm better than someone else might have, for reasons ranging from more resources to political systems to your social network, you can feel a sense of survivor's guilt or thriver's guilt.

This exercise will help you gain clarity on your own sense of guilt, so that you can harness it to grow and potentially help others. Use the space provided to reflect on the following questions:

- What exactly do you feel guilty about?
- How does this play out in your life? For instance, what thoughts or feelings are you plagued by, and what triggers them?
- How do you punish yourself? (People punish themselves in ways they can be unaware of when they experience survivor's or thriver's guilt. This could be in the form of self-sabotage behaviors, denying joy, or excessive self-criticism.)
- Is there anyone who actively criticizes you or puts you down for your privilege?
- If you feel lucky that you have better resources, how have you designed your life to a point where you are currently relatively cushioned?
- Were these "cushions" provided by someone else? Consider your gratitude for how that person helped you.
- How can you give back, and support someone else who may be in a less privileged position?

Understanding Why This Matters

There are times when people who are considered more privileged are criticized. This can amp up the survivor's or thriver's guilt you already feel—which harms your mental and physical health even more. The truth is, you don't need to suffer more in order to make someone else feel less bad. Making yourself more miserable only kicks off a pointless race to the bottom.

Connecting with What Matters

Here's what this exercise has taught me about my guilt:

_____

_____

_____

_____

_____

Here's how I see my guilt differently now:

_____

_____

_____

_____

_____

Taking Action on What Matters

1. Whenever you feel guilty, redo the exercises Assign Colors to Your Emotions and Reset Your Brain in this chapter. They will help you to process what's going on, so you regain control of your thoughts and feelings.
2. Continue to tap in to gratitude for how you have created the life you have, and for how others have helped you get there. Gratitude is an easy (and free!) booster for your health.
3. Then, think about what you could do for an individual, a group, or a cause. How could you best use your resources—such as time, money, or energy—right now?

RITUALIZING SUCCESS

You maximize success by getting clear on the journey, which is what you'll do in this exercise. First, you'll identify rewards, so your brain gets that feel-good dopamine boost whenever you do what you set out to do. Next, you'll figure out what stands in your way, so you're not surprised, but rather prepared to tackle these obstacles head-on. Then, you'll set mini-milestones so you can check in with yourself to ensure you're on track and practicing your new skills and habits without needlessly second-guessing yourself.

Rewarding Myself

I'll reward myself when I reach these mini-milestones:

_____

_____

_____

_____

Here's how I'll reward myself: (include both small and big rewards)

_____

_____

_____

_____

Identifying Obstacles

These are the factors that might make this journey more difficult:

_____

_____

_____

_____

Here's what I can do to get around these challenges:

_____

_____

_____

_____

These are the beliefs that stand in my way:

_____

_____

_____

_____

_____

Here's what I can do to get around these beliefs:

_____

_____

_____

_____

_____

Checking In

Here's how long I'll dedicate to discovering what matters to me right now: _____

I will check in with myself every _____ .

Putting It All Together

Now that you've filled out the previous sections, integrate them here. Then, set these review dates in your calendar:

Date:	Goal:
Date:	Milestone:
Date:	Milestone:
Date:	Milestone:
Where I am now:	

CHAPTER 3

Discovering What Matters in Your Relationships

Healthy, supportive, and intimate relationships help you thrive; toxic or superficial relationships where you feel lonely or hurt harm you mentally and physically, no matter how many of these relationships you have. Part of forming and nurturing a good relationship is first considering who you are in the relationship, what you can give to it, and what you need from the relationship. And it's equally important to consider what you *don't* want or *won't* support in a relationship.

In this chapter, you will determine the things you need and want from your connections with other people, as well as what you don't need or want, and boundaries that will keep you safe and happy. Then you'll run an "audit" on your social life, diagnosing the current health of your relationships and deciding which relationships need a change or should be reconsidered. It's time to reclaim the energy you've been losing to unhealthy bonds and give it back to what matters to you in your relationships.

SETTING INTENTIONS AND GOALS

To support your success in the exercises that follow, answer these questions about your intentions and goals for this chapter.

I want to feel _____ about my relationships.

As I discover what matters in my relationships, I want to become the type of person who _____

_____ .

This is what I want to accomplish from discovering what matters in my relationships:	These are the mini-milestones I'm breaking this larger goal into:
_____	_____
_____	_____
_____	_____
_____	_____
_____	_____
_____	_____
_____	_____
_____	_____
_____	_____
_____	_____
_____	_____
_____	_____
_____	_____
_____	_____
_____	_____

IDENTIFY YOUR PSYCHOLOGICAL SAFETY NEEDS

In every interaction we have, we either meet or withhold someone else's "psychological safety" needs. Think back to a time when you didn't feel you could voice your real opinion or make a suggestion, even if someone else said they wanted to hear it. Maybe you had the words but not the confidence that it was the right place or time to share them; you were afraid your honesty would backfire. Now remember a time when you knew that even though your opinion or suggestion might be initially difficult for the other person or group to hear, you could still say it, and you'd all grow because of it. The difference between these scenarios is that in the second situation, you have psychological safety.

The SCARF model breaks down your psychological safety needs into five main parts: status, certainty, autonomy, relatedness, and fairness. Everyone prioritizes these needs differently. Read through the descriptions of these needs and then rank them from 1–5, in order of what means the most to you—1 being the least important and 5 being the most important.

_____   Status: People with high status needs like to feel respected and acknowledged for their contributions, talents, and possessions. They may sometimes be more sensitive to perceiving that they are not respected or acknowledged for these things. They might also take things personally or mistakenly believe that they are being picked on.

_____   Certainty: People with high certainty needs shine best when they are told what to do and are given structure in tasks, expectations, etc. They also appreciate regular check-ins, so they know they are heading in the right direction. Being expected to guess the nuances in others' words or come up with the steps between the start and the end goal of a task can cause them anxiety.

_____ Autonomy: People with high autonomy needs love being able to control their tasks and their environments, and they also appreciate being given the freedom to do so. This helps them to feel trusted, and they grow from the responsibility they are given. When they are micromanaged, their autonomy needs are threatened.

_____ Relatedness: People with high relatedness needs appreciate harmony in relationships. When everyone's objectives and actions are aligned, they feel psychologically safe because this creates a sense of belonging. In contrast, they dislike conflict and asserting themselves, even if maintaining the false harmony costs them.

_____ Fairness: People with high fairness needs like justice and equity. For instance, praise and privilege should be given to those who deserve them. They are sensitive to scenarios when bad behaviors are not addressed, and when freeloaders are rewarded.

Understanding Why This Matters

When you understand your own and others' psychological safety needs, you are better able to respond to these needs, which in turn helps cultivate authentic and effective relationships. When your psychological safety needs are not met, your brain produces a threat response, and your adrenaline levels increase. This makes you less rational and more negative, and reduces your effectiveness at planning, collaborating, and/or focusing.

Your brain instinctively responds to social threats and rewards in the same way it responds to physical threats and rewards. People gravitate toward safe relationships because these create a sense of reward. In contrast, they avoid psychologically unsafe relationships because these foster a sense of social threat. You're likeliest to feel threatened and shut down when your top two psychological safety needs are not met. And you're likeliest to accidentally threaten someone else whose top two psychological safety needs correspond with your least-prioritized ones.

It's easy to understand which of your relationships are psychologically safe and which are not. If you want to improve the psychological safety of a relationship, figuring out exactly what your differing needs are will teach you what you can do differently to effectively communicate your needs and meet other people's needs.

Connecting with What Matters

These are my top two psychological safety needs:

1. _____
_____
_____

2. _____
_____
_____

These are my two least important safety needs:

1. _____
_____
_____

2. _____
_____
_____

These are the people who haven't been able to meet my needs:

_____
_____
_____
_____
_____
_____

These are the people whose needs I may not be meeting:

_____
_____
_____
_____
_____
_____

Now that you've reflected on your needs and the needs of the people close to you, it will benefit your relationships when you can ask for what gives you psychological safety, and be thoughtful about giving similar considerations to those who value your least-prioritized needs. Here is what to ask for or give based on each need:

- Status: Praise for accomplishments, credit to contributions, and notice for what you/they are proud of. This would be especially useful in a group context.
- Certainty: Regular check-ins, explicit steps, and a paraphrasing of what you've both agreed upon to make sure you're on the same page. Ask or tell them what extent of clarity is needed.
- Autonomy: Trust with the control of tasks or to make decisions. You can agree on the start, midpoint, and end point beforehand. Also, check in on what "micromanaging" means to you both.
- Relatedness: Check-ins on how you/they are feeling and what you/they are thinking, in order to feel connected and bonded to the relationship or group.
- Fairness: Address unfair behavior or undeserving rewards, especially in a group setting. Have mutually agreed-upon expectations and goals in a relationship, and allow space for open and honest communication to discuss your/their thought process behind the decisions you/they make.

DIAGNOSE THE HEALTH OF YOUR RELATIONSHIPS

Healthy relationships are like vitamins for your well-being. And it takes two to tango: Both people need to be considerate, respectful, and kind, acting in consistently healthy ways. Of course, sometimes one of you may drop the ball. Sometimes this pattern may even persist unintentionally. This is okay (and normal), as long as you can come together to repair what's gone wrong. Healing the relationship, bringing it back to a healthy place, will strengthen both parties and improve the relationship as a whole, making it a win-win-win. This exercise invites you to reflect on unhealthy behaviors, so you can start weeding out what's hurting your relationships or let go of a relationship that is no longer aligned to what matters to you.

If you think of red flags as the clear no-go zones, and green flags as signs that it's clear to keep going, then amber flags make you pause and wonder if a certain behavior was deliberate. The following are amber and red flags in relationships. Use the space provided to reflect on whether these are things you do, or things someone else does, and how often they occur (and how they make you feel). Use the next exercise in this chapter to help you reflect on the boundaries section.

Respect

- Someone makes everything about them.
- Someone shames others for their actions or thoughts.
- Someone mocks others, says "I told you so," or rubs salt on wounds.
- Someone reminds others of how much worse off they used to be, in order to keep the others feeling small.
- Someone gives backhanded compliments and/or makes passive-aggressive remarks.
- Someone apologizes too much.
- Someone never apologizes, or not sincerely.
- Someone always insists on their way.

_____

_____

_____

_____

Commitment

- Someone constantly cancels at the last minute.
- Someone is consistently late.
- Someone makes offers they don't follow through on.

_____

_____

_____

Communication

- Someone tends to overexplain.
- Someone jumps in to complete others' sentences, to the point of frustration.
- Someone listens too much, and does not share.

- Someone jumps in to talk, and does not listen.

_____

_____

Celebrating Each Other

- Someone never lets others take the limelight, even when deserved.
- Someone never steps up to the spotlight.

- Someone never thanks the other (sincerely).
- Someone takes all the credit.

_____

_____

_____

Boundaries

- Someone expects others to listen to all their problems.
- Someone treats the relationship as a place to be rescued or pitied.
- Someone asks intrusive questions.

- Someone doesn't know how to say no to uncomfortable questions.

_____

_____

- Someone gives unsolicited advice and/or opinions.
- Someone gives advice solely based on their own experiences, not what's good for the other party.
- Someone gets upset when the other party does not follow their advice.

- Someone needs to always be right.
- Someone gives no room for compromise.
- Personal attacks are thrown into advice or opinions.

_____

_____

_____

_____

Understanding Why This Matters

The health—or lack of health—of a relationship builds up over time. Sometimes, it's you. Sometimes, it's them. Additionally, if you realize you act in a particular way you're not proud of with certain people, then it may be the relationship dynamics themselves that are causing that to happen.

When you examine these potential amber and red flags honestly, you can then decide which relationships are worth doing something about—either making a change to your own behaviors or communicating about a change you need from the other person—and which no longer have a place in your life.

Of course, it is good to be understanding of why people do what they do, but when you continue to let things slide, you are actually condoning the bad behavior. And you forget to be sympathetic and empathetic toward yourself in the process. This harms your mental and physical health more than you might be aware of. Resentment builds up, hurting even those relationships that started healthy, or with a lot of potential to be healthy.

Connecting with What Matters

Here's what I learned about
myself in doing this exercise:

_____

_____

_____

_____

_____

_____

_____

_____

_____

_____

This exercise made me feel:

_____

_____

_____

_____

These are patterns I've
noticed about myself in
relationships:

_____

_____

_____

_____

_____

Taking Action on What Matters

1. **Take stock of your relationships:**

These are your own relationship patterns that need to change, and why:

_____

_____

_____

_____

_____

These are the relationships that would benefit from open, honest discussion about what needs to change on the part of the other person in order to make the relationship healthier:

_____

_____

These are the relationships that need to go:

_____

_____

2. What can you do differently?

Next, use the space provided to consider the things that you could do differently. Here are some example scenarios and possible alternative behaviors:

- Instead of overexplaining, you could say, "You look curious, what would you like to know? I'll answer what I feel comfortable with."
- If you forget to thank them and/or often point out what's going wrong, you could instead give specific and sincere thanks for when something goes right. This will encourage more of these positive behaviors.
- Instead of jumping in to speak while they are still talking, curl your toes slowly, so you get back into your body and away from your overactive brain. Remind yourself that the best communication isn't about sounding smart or "winning" but about responding to what the other person is really saying. That means taking in everything, from their words to their body language.
- If you tend to give unsolicited advice, start by asking, "What would you like from this? A listening ear, or someone to work through a solution with you?"

_____

_____

_____

_____

INSTALL STRONG, GRACEFUL BOUNDARIES

Most people have some idea of the specific things they want from relationships and how to ask for them, but many don't know the other side of the equation: *boundaries*. Psychotherapist Terri Cole says that boundaries are the guidebook that you write to teach people how to treat you. They are the important no's in your life—what you won't tolerate—and the limits you set for each unique situation or relationship. If you expect people to read your mind or hope they suddenly stop doing something that upsets you without prompting, you'll be disappointed and even resentful.

In this exercise, you'll consider the different aspects of boundaries in your life, so you're clear on how you'd like to be treated.

1. Reflect on your boundaries in these areas:

Physical boundaries:

These include your body and your personal space, like who's not allowed to barge into your bedroom.

_____

_____

_____

_____

Mental boundaries:

The right to have your thoughts, opinions, and values, without someone else forcing their ideas on you.

_____

_____

_____

_____

Sexual boundaries:

What kinds of sexual encounters are acceptable with whom, where, and when; and what you will not consent to.

_____

_____

_____

_____

Material boundaries:

Whether someone can access your possessions, and under what conditions.

_____

_____

_____

_____

Time boundaries:

Who you'll allow access to your time, and when they will be allowed to access that time.

_____

_____

_____

_____

Emotional boundaries:

Not giving you unsolicited advice or criticism, blaming you for how they feel, or expecting you to share (or hear) intimate details.

_____

_____

_____

_____

2. **Reflect on the boundaries in your closest relationships:**

The people who are:

Mostly respectful, and how:	Sometimes respectful, and how:	Disrespectful of my boundaries, and how:
_____	_____	_____
_____	_____	_____
_____	_____	_____
_____	_____	_____
_____	_____	_____
_____	_____	_____
_____	_____	_____
_____	_____	_____
_____	_____	_____
_____	_____	_____
_____	_____	_____
_____	_____	_____

3. **Now consider which of the following statements apply to you:**

☐   I feel comfortable accepting or asking for help.

☐   I know when and who to share what information with.

☐   I know how to say no firmly.

☐   I say no when necessary, even if I know it's not being "nice."

☐   When I say no, I don't need to overexplain or make someone feel bad for it.

☐   I respect my thoughts, values, and opinions.

☐   Even when I or someone close is in dire need of emotional support, I give myself space to respond instead of jumping in.

☐   I refuse to take on others' problems.

☐   I do not tolerate disrespectful behavior.

☐   I understand that sometimes people will say no, and I can deal with that.

These statements are hallmarks of healthy boundaries, and you may want to work on the ones that don't currently apply to you.

Understanding Why This Matters

Many people worry that having boundaries will make them seem confrontational or cold. The truth is, you can express your boundaries gracefully, in a way that is ultimately more kind for the relationship than letting upset feelings fester. Your "no" is just as important as your "yes."

Not having boundaries can also lead to "empathy burnout." It's easy to try to understand why some people do disrespectful things or are emotionally needy, and attempt to explain away behaviors that disregard boundaries. However, your brain starts to fuse that person with yourself, and you become fatigued. Often, you may even find yourself having empathy for others at the cost of empathy for yourself.

Sometimes, you might run into what Terri Cole calls "boundary destroyers." These are people who persistently and deliberately trample all over your boundaries because they feel entitled to, or they like watching the upset that comes from it. When you identify who falls into this category and release the relationships that only serve to hurt you, you can reserve your energy for yourself and those who truly matter to your happiest, most fulfilled life.

Connecting with What Matters

Here's how I felt about boundaries before doing this exercise:

_____

_____

_____

_____

_____

Here's what I've learned about myself in the process:

_____

_____

_____

_____

_____

Taking Action on What Matters

1. List the boundaries that you most urgently need to put in place:

_____

_____

_____

_____

_____

_____

_____

_____

_____

_____

Here are the benefits of setting these boundaries:

_____

_____

_____

_____

Here are the costs of not setting these boundaries:

_____

_____

_____

_____

2. **Identify mindsets that might keep you from setting appropriate boundaries:**

This could include "boundaries make me a bad/cold person." As you practice setting boundaries, you'll find that these mindsets will pop up to stand in your way. Being aware of them as old beliefs that don't serve you will help you to let go of them and move forward.

_____

_____

_____

3. **Identify skills that will help build boundaries:**

People often find it hard to establish boundaries because they lack the necessary skills to do so or believe they don't have permission to set emotional limits. Relevant emotional skills include what to say and when to say it.

_____

_____

_____

4. **Create a conversation:**

The easiest way to set a boundary is to write a script for what you will say, memorize it, and then have the talk with whomever that boundary involves. The script should include:

- **Setting the scene:** "I notice that when we interact, we have this pattern: [pattern]."
- **Getting clear:** "When you do [behavior], I feel [emotion]."
- **Request:** "I'd like you to stop this from now on."
- **Invite conversation:** "What do you think?"

Most people will apologize for behavior they weren't aware was disrespectful. Observe if this person sticks to their word going forward, or if they are willing to make amends should they occasionally slip back to the boundary-breaching behavior.

IDENTIFY AND GIVE YOUR AMBIVALENT RELATIONSHIPS THE BOOT

People often think it's the toxic relationships that are the most hazardous for them. Really it's the ambivalent relationships that can harm your well-being the most. Because ambivalent relationships are high in both positive *and* negative interactions, their harmfulness is not as obvious. This gray zone is where these relationships are born and bred.

Read the following signs of ambivalent relationships and consider to what extent these apply to your relationships.

- Never-ending drama: While everyone goes through life's ups and downs, the ambivalent friend's life feels like a never-ending train wreck. They may tend to blame the world or other people.
- Making you feel bad for having feelings: You'll often hear "I'm sorry you feel this way," which *sounds* like they are validating your feelings but is really a passive-aggressive way of putting the blame on you for feeling the way you do, instead of on them for doing whatever upset you.
- Incredibly self-absorbed: Even if they listen, it's only to find a way to hijack the spotlight. It's a big, loud story, or why they've got it worse than you—an exhausting competition you didn't sign up for.
- Draining: You are exhausted after an interaction with them.
- Confusing: Because there are some positive aspects, you try to justify spending more time with them. You're driven by guilt or obligation, even if you're unsure if you enjoy hanging out with them.

Understanding Why This Matters

It's easy to equate the length of your relationship with how deep (and rewarding) it actually is, and people can often defend the ambivalent relationship because of its longevity. The problem is, you spend significant resources on people who don't have your back or bring you real joy.

Here are the relationships I have
identified as ambivalent:

_____

_____

_____

_____

_____

_____

_____

Here's what I've learned about
myself or my relationships from
doing this exercise:

_____

_____

_____

_____

_____

_____

Taking Action on What Matters

1. Reflect on each ambivalent relationship:

First, draw up a balance sheet of the pros and cons of each ambivalent relationship (use the following chart to help), without considering the length of the relationship. Deep, rational reflection will help you face reality head-on.

RELATIONSHIP:	
Pros:	Cons:

2. Decide what you'd like to do with each relationship:

Now decide how you'd like to end things or keep your distance. If the person is dramatic and often bombards you, then it might not be worth saying anything; just stop responding to their communications. For others, you might enforce a clear boundary by telling them you'd like to end things.

Here is how I will respond to ambivalent relationships:

_____

_____

_____

_____

_____

_____

3. Reflect on how to reroute energy:

Finally, with this energy freed up, consider how you can reroute it to yourself and the people you care about who treat you the way you deserve.

Here is how I will use my freed energy:

_____

_____

_____

_____

_____

_____

RECLAIM YOUR SOCIAL ENERGY

Being plugged into your devices 24/7 is convenient, true, but it's also exhausting and places undue pressure on you to always be connected. There is a never-ending, overwhelming stream of comments, messages, and information to sift through. And honestly, you don't have to answer everything or everyone, or be the last person to say something in a conversation—that's an invisible energy depleter you can definitely kick to the curb.

1. **Assess your communications**
   Here are some prompts to help you decide what and whom you'd like to respond to.

These are the people I'll prioritize answering:

_____

_____

_____

_____

These are the communications or topics I will answer:

_____

_____

_____

_____

These are the people I don't need to answer:

_____

_____

_____

_____

These are the communications or topics I don't need to answer:

_____

_____

_____

_____

If I stopped answering these people and things...

Here's how I'd feel worse:

_____

_____

_____

_____

But here's how I'd feel better:

_____

_____

_____

_____

2. Review your contacts list

Does it have numbers of people you don't even know or never communicate with?

Here's what qualifies someone to be in my contacts list:

_____

_____

_____

3. Assess notifications

Notifications pinging nonstop on your phone distract you and burn your energy. To start reclaiming control, answer the following prompts.

These are the apps where notifications are justifiable:	These notifications are unnecessary or only sometimes necessary: (e.g., during versus after-work hours)	Here's when my phone can be muted:
_____		_____
_____	_____	_____
_____	_____	_____
_____	_____	_____
_____	_____	_____
_____	_____	_____
_____	_____	_____
_____	_____	_____
_____	_____	_____
_____	_____	_____

Notifications and that constant urge to keep replying out of habit, or because you think you should, make you less engaged in the present moment. You switch your attention back and forth across different conversations, future considerations, etc., meaning that your focus is divided. In contrast, being present, focusing on what is actually happening right now in front of you, has better outcomes for your life, work, and relationships. You give these things your all, instead of distracted effort.

Connecting with What Matters

Here's what I've realized about how much social energy I needlessly waste:

_____

_____

_____

_____

_____

Here's what surprised me most:

_____

_____

_____

_____

_____

Taking Action on What Matters

First, commit to what you've identified in the previous section. Turn off all unnecessary notifications, clean up your contacts list, and put your rules of whom and what to respond to somewhere you will see them regularly as you build this new discipline.

Schedule in reviews of these rules so you can adjust them according to how well they are working for you, and determine what you'd like to do even better.

IDENTIFY WHO YOU'LL SAY WHAT TO

A key part of relationships is knowing what—and how much—to say to whom. Sometimes, when you give too much information without considering boundaries, you can make people uncomfortable. You may not do this intentionally but because you were nervous and rambling, or felt so comfortable, you forgot to think before speaking. Or, people may feel you don't share enough, and think you are withholding information or aren't committed to the relationship because you are never vulnerable with them. In short, sharing details willy-nilly is as hazardous as keeping mum. Sometimes, you just get it right, if you're lucky or in sync with the other person. But why not get it right more often, by investing time to figure out how to show up better in your relationships?

This exercise helps you get clarity on the levels of closeness in your relationships. The closer the person, the more intimate and vulnerable the details shared. First, you'll decide what qualifies a person to be at a certain level. Then, you'll decide what topics are appropriate to talk about at that level. Finally, you will match people in your life to these criteria. Feel free to add levels as you go to tailor the exercise to your experiences.

LEVEL 1—Strangers

The types of people here:	The topics I can talk about:	The people in my life who belong here:
_____	_____	_____
_____	_____	_____
_____	_____	_____
_____	_____	_____
_____	_____	_____
_____	_____	_____
_____	_____	_____

LEVEL 2—Acquaintances

The types of people here:	The topics I can talk about:	The people in my life who belong here:
_____	_____	_____
_____	_____	_____
_____	_____	_____
_____	_____	_____
_____	_____	_____
_____	_____	_____
_____	_____	_____

The qualities about them that qualify them to be here:

_____

_____

The qualities about the relationship that qualify them to be here:

_____

_____

LEVEL 3—Colleagues and newer friends

The types of people here:	The topics I can talk about:	The people in my life who belong here:
_____	_____	_____
_____	_____	_____
_____	_____	_____
_____	_____	_____
_____	_____	_____
_____	_____	_____

The qualities about them that qualify them to be here:

_____

_____

The qualities about the relationship that qualify them to be here:

_____

_____

LEVEL 4—Very close friends, family, mentors

The types of people here:	The topics I can talk about:	The people in my life who belong here:
_____	_____	_____
_____	_____	_____
_____	_____	_____
_____	_____	_____
_____	_____	_____
_____	_____	_____
_____	_____	_____

The qualities about them that qualify them to be here:

_____

_____

The qualities about the relationship that qualify them to be here:

_____

_____

The types of people here:

The topics I can talk about:

The people in my life who belong here:

_____

_____

_____

_____

_____

_____

_____

_____

_____

_____

_____

_____

_____

_____

_____

The qualities about them that qualify them to be here:

_____

_____

The qualities about the relationship that qualify them to be here:

_____

_____

Understanding Why This Matters

Most people go through life never thinking about what to say to whom. This lack of thoughtfulness means some relationships are a game of hits and misses—maybe some acquaintances who have passed you by could have blossomed to a deeper level of friendship if you'd been more intentional with your words in the beginning. The only thing you can really control in a relationship is how you act, and in that, you influence the quality of the interaction. By reflecting honestly on who you can say what to, you know you've played your part toward allowing that relationship to reach its full potential.

Another benefit of this exercise is confidence. Sometimes, you second-guess yourself, wondering if it's appropriate to say something. In close relationships, some degree of vulnerability is needed, because that's how people connect. In others, that level of detail is perceived as too much information, because the relationship simply isn't ready for that depth of intimacy. When unsure, you're likely to overthink, and are less likely to fully engage in the interaction. Being confident about who to say what to can prevent this.

You also learn how much you invest in each relationship by getting clear on what qualifies someone to be at a certain level. After all, your time and energy are finite and a privilege you gift someone. How you spend that time and energy matters. This exercise also draws attention to how a certain person has progressed across the different levels, whether they become closer to or further from you.

Connecting with What Matters

Here's what I've learned about my relationships from this exercise:

_____

_____

_____

_____

_____

_____

_____

_____

Here's what I've learned about myself in relationships from this exercise:

_____

_____

_____

This is how the exercise made me feel:

_____

_____

_____

1. Assess

First, use the following space to map out your own levels of closeness like an onion, with the Innermost Level in the center.

2. Reflect

Next, reflect on the following prompts. This isn't about assigning blame, but rather noticing the insights you gain from reflection that will help you take more control over your part in different relationships.

I am...   Here's why:

☐ happy   _____
☐ feeling neutral   _____
☐ unhappy   _____

with my circles of intimacy.   _____

This is what I've realized I've been doing right so far:

_____

_____

_____

_____

This is what I've realized I could be doing better:

_____

_____

_____

_____

This is the level of intimacy that needs the most change:

_____

_____

_____

_____

Here are the most pressing changes needed:

_____

_____

_____

_____

3. Plan

Armed with these insights, you are ready to create an action plan. Maybe it's to commit to being more vulnerable with a certain person at your deepest level, talking more about intimate topics. Or perhaps it's to commit to restraining yourself with another person in an outer level. Or you might feel you need more people at a certain level, and decide to make more new friends.

These are the three action steps I'll commit to:

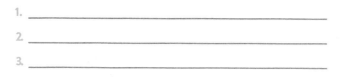

1. _____

2. _____

3. _____

LEARN HOW TO MAKE FASCINATING SMALL TALK

Bestselling author Ramit Sethi likens small talk to part of the ritual of life. He says that you don't go to a fancy restaurant, gobble your food, and rush out. That's just not how the experience is meant to be. Similarly, small talk is part of the experience of meeting people and having relationships. The problem, however, is that it can feel so dull and trivial. But what if your small talk was so fascinating that even the people who dislike small talk most would engage heartily in it? Meaning, you easily connect with new people and strengthen bonds in older relationships, rather than let your dislike of small talk keep you isolated.

This exercise invites you to test out better small-talk topics and create your own questions for sparking interesting small talk. These questions are inspired by the legendary Proust Questionnaire, Arthur Aron's "36 Questions That Lead to Love," and Alexandra Franzen's "100 Questions to Spark Conversation and Connection."

Light questions:

- What's the best thing that happened to you today?
- What's one thing that's impacted you recently?
- What made you show up today?

Easy questions about the other person:

- Do you identify as an introvert, extrovert, or ambivert?
- How would your best friend introduce you to a stranger?
- How do you spend your days?

Interesting questions that make people think:

- If you could invite anyone living or dead to a dinner party, which three guests would you invite? And why?
- What's your favorite journey you've ever taken? And why?

Understanding Why This Matters

Most small talk revolves around the weather, where you live, and what you do for work. There's only so much you can talk about with the first two topics, and not everybody works. Asking different questions piques curiosity, so both parties listen deeper. This encourages a sense of connection, without the risk of crossing boundaries or giving too much information.

Connecting with What Matters

Here's how I used to feel about small talk before this exercise:

_____

_____

_____

_____

_____

Here's how I see small talk differently now:

_____

_____

_____

_____

_____

Taking Action on What Matters

Think about your own responses to these questions, or check out the referenced lists of questions. Chances are, you may not have considered these subjects and you'll learn something about yourself. You may also craft questions that suit your style more.

It may feel strange asking these questions at first. Start with the lightest ones, and use the others to branch off something that the person says. Last, remember that the people who make small talk look effortless have practiced it—use each opportunity to refine your skills in having fascinating conversations.

CULTIVATE DEEPER INTIMACY

Relationships don't get deeper and more intimate with time; it's effort and vulnerability that create the magic. This exercise invites you to try two ways to cultivate deeper intimacy: First, by practicing *mitfreude*, or sharing in someone's joy, and second, by asking questions that make people think and share deeply. As in the previous exercise, these questions are inspired by the Proust Questionnaire, Arthur Aron's "36 Questions That Lead to Love," and Alexandra Franzen's "100 Questions to Spark Conversation and Connection."

First, reflect on how you respond when people you're close to share good news. You could have a mixture of feelings and responses, depending on who's sharing and what's going on in your life at that time.

Here is how I respond to good news:

_____

_____

_____

_____

Or maybe you're more likely to be there for someone during their hard times rather than their joyful times.

Consider why this may be so:

_____

_____

_____

_____

What gets in the way of you fully sharing in someone else's joy?

_____

_____

_____

_____

What could you do differently, going forward, to better share in another person's joy?

_____

_____

_____

_____

Next, here are some questions you could ask to get the other person (and yourself) thinking and sharing on a deeper level:

- What is your idea of perfect happiness?
- When was the last time you astonished yourself?
- If you could choose your life obstacles, would you keep the ones you have?
- What are you most grateful for, right now?
- If you were a perfume, what scents would you be made of?
- If you could sit down with your thirteen-year-old self, what would you tell them?

Understanding Why This Matters

Your intimate relationships grow stronger when you share each other's joys—even more so than when you support each other through hard times. This is a skill few know about, so go easy on yourself as you cultivate it.

Asking deeper questions offers people an opportunity to reflect deeply and invites them to reveal who they are to themselves *and* to you. This way, your interactions become a great time to bond.

Here's what I've learned about the way I am there for people through good and bad times:

_____

_____

_____

_____

_____

_____

_____

_____

Here's how I feel about asking deeper questions:

_____

_____

_____

_____

_____

_____

_____

_____

Taking Action on What Matters

The next time someone has good news to share, and you find yourself stuck in your own head, take a moment to curl your toes slowly so you become more engaged with what's going on. Then remind yourself that this is about them, and you want to nourish your relationship. Tell them specifically what you feel happy or proud of them for, and do something to celebrate together.

For the questions, organize an event like a dinner party, or simply tell someone close to you that you'd love to try out this exercise.

RITUALIZING SUCCESS

You maximize success by getting clear on the journey, which is what you'll do in this exercise. First, you'll identify rewards, so your brain gets that feel-good dopamine boost whenever you do what you set out to do. Next, you'll figure out what stands in your way, so you're not surprised, but rather prepared to tackle these obstacles head-on. Then, you'll set mini-milestones so you can check in with yourself to ensure you're on track and practicing your new skills and habits without needlessly second-guessing yourself.

Rewarding Myself

I'll reward myself when I reach these mini-milestones:

_____

_____

_____

_____

Here's how I'll reward myself: (include both small and big rewards)

_____

_____

_____

_____

Identifying Obstacles

These are the factors that might make this journey more difficult:

_____

_____

_____

_____

Here's what I can do to get around these challenges:

_____

_____

_____

_____

These are the beliefs that stand in my way:

_____

_____

_____

_____

Here's what I can do to get around these beliefs:

_____

_____

_____

_____

Checking In

Here's how long I'll dedicate to discovering what matters to me right now: _____

I will check in with myself every _____ .

Putting It All Together

Now that you've filled out the previous sections, integrate them here. Then, set these review dates in your calendar:

Date:	Goal:
Date:	Milestone:
Date:	Milestone:
Date:	Milestone:
Where I am now:	

CHAPTER 4

Discovering What Matters in Your Home

Is your home lived-in or staged? Loved or neglected? Does it look neat and organized from the outside but like a hot mess inside? You spend a substantial chunk of your life at home. Even if you travel or work away often, home is that safe space where you recharge and sleep. In short, it is an intimate place that deserves to be treated with respect.

In this chapter, you will consider how your home can nourish you, beyond being a functional roof over your head. You will examine the different elements you can play with to achieve a space that fosters the best of what matters to you. Of course, clutter and the unwanted emotions stored in objects often get in the way, and this chapter invites you to clean things up and toss out what doesn't matter. You will learn how to set up your home for success—so it's easier for you to grow the habits you've always wanted, and design better mornings and nights. You'll also look at organizing your digital home—all of your technological devices—and get to know your home city better.

SETTING INTENTIONS AND GOALS

To support your success in the exercises that follow, answer these questions about your intentions and goals for this chapter.

I want to feel_____ about my home.

As I discover what matters in my home, I want to become the type of person who_____

_____

This is what I want to accomplish from discovering what matters in my home:

These are the mini-milestones I'm breaking this larger goal into:

LEARN TO LET YOUR HOME NOURISH YOU

Architects, designers, and feng shui practitioners all agree that your relationship with your home environment defines how you feel and live. In other words, love your home, and it will love you back. Often, people wait to escape to vacations or weekend homes to be in an environment they love. That only widens the divide between the escape and home, making you less and less satisfied with your living space—and your life. What if you could feel inspired, safe, and supported every day, by making small tweaks to your current surroundings?

This exercise breaks down your home into six main elements, including light and sound. As you review each element, make notes about what you'd like in your own space.

1. Light:

Lots of sunlight during the day and then three different sources of warm lighting in the evenings, so you don't rely on harsh overhead lights.

_____

_____

_____

_____

2. Scent:

Different scents (e.g., diffused essential oils, home fragrances, and candles) can help you be more productive, connected, or relaxed.

_____

_____

_____

_____

3. Temperature:

Consider what temperature makes you feel comfortable in each season.

_____

_____

_____

4. Sound:

Is your home too loud or too quiet? If you love music, are you making time to play it?

_____

_____

_____

5. **Life:**
   Plants, pets, and fresh-cut flowers can bring life to your house. How would these fit with your lifestyle?

_____

_____

_____

_____

6. **Beauty:**
   What are your needs for beauty in the form of design, furniture, art, and mementos?

_____

_____

_____

_____

Understanding Why This Matters

Everyone has a dream home. Some may have the privilege of being able to remodel or create that dream when they move. But even if you don't have those kinds of resources, you don't have to wait for that mythical "some day" to thoughtfully design your surroundings. You can design a life where you walk into a home you love.

Connecting with What Matters

I've had these insights about how I'd like my home to be:

_____

_____

_____

_____

_____

_____

I've learned that I already love these things about my home:

_____

_____

_____

_____

_____

_____

Taking Action on What Matters

Based on the preferences you've identified, first consider how you'd incorporate them into your existing space. This could include what you'd like to add, replace, or remove for each element, like swapping out white lights for warmer halogen bulbs, including a few live plants in your living room, or tossing a rug that's past its prime. And if something is unrealistic right now, what's a good alternative? A new white carpet might not be best with pets or young kids, but a darker shade or a printed carpet could still make the space feel welcoming. Next, create an action plan for improving your home in the far right column.

Light:

_____

_____

_____

_____

Scent:

_____

_____

_____

_____

Temperature:

_____

_____

_____

_____

Sound:

_____

_____

_____

_____

Life:

_____

_____

_____

_____

Beauty:

_____

_____

_____

_____

What are the logistics involved?

_____

_____

_____

_____

_____

_____

Would you work according to element or room?

_____

_____

_____

_____

_____

_____

CREATE SPACE FOR YOUR FUTURE

British artist William Morris said, "Have nothing in your house that you do not know to be useful, or believe to be beautiful." The things you own carry specific energies that affect how you feel and connect you to specific times in your life. Because of this, they can become "emotional clutter," influencing you to live in the past. This exercise invites you to ask specific questions about your possessions, which will help you prioritize what you own (and want to own), focusing on what is useful and makes you feel good.

For each category, reflect on the thoughts that come to mind and the obvious items to keep or throw away.

"Is this useful?"

Items here are relevant to your life; you actually use them fairly regularly. Compare these to things you imagined you'd use someday and never did, or something you've outgrown. If you're saving relevant items here for record-keeping purposes—like receipts and documents—you may digitize them and toss the physical versions.

_____

_____

_____

_____

"Is this a good kind of sentimental?"

Sometimes people hold on to things from their past, confusing nostalgia with haunting ghosts. Your possessions trigger emotions, so keep only what evokes good feelings. If it's part of a larger collection, you may keep a few items, and maybe photograph the rest before tossing them. Or, turn your favorite bits into an art project.

_____

_____

_____

_____

"Do I like/want it?"

Maybe the item is not obviously useful or nostalgic, but it's something you really like, such as art.

_____

_____

_____

_____

Understanding Why This Matters

It's too easy for things to pile up at home, and this clutter can feel heavy physically and emotionally. When every given space is occupied, it can literally feel like there's no room to breathe. That's why it's important to recognize why you hold on to some things, and to release unhelpful feelings like regret as you let go of these items. Being thoughtful about your possessions creates space for a future filled with what matters.

Connecting with What Matters

Here's what I've learned from this exercise about the things I accumulate at home:

_____

_____

_____

_____

_____

_____

Here's why I allow things to pile up:

_____

_____

_____

_____

_____

_____

1. **Assess how you want to organize/display your things:**
   Now that you've picked what to keep, consider how you need to organize or display these things. Adopt the mindset of a curator—you admire art in galleries because there is negative space between the works. You might decide to keep some in storage, and rotate what's displayed seasonally—you can even track what's stored where in a spreadsheet.

   Here is how I will organize/display my things:

   _____

   _____

   _____

   _____

   _____

2. **Assess the system you will use for future things:**
   Also, create a system for choosing what enters and/or stays in your house. For instance, you could ban all receipts or recycle all packaging. Or implement a "one item in, one item out" rule.

   I will use the following system to ensure each item has a purpose in my home:

   _____

   _____

   _____

   _____

   _____

   _____

EMOTIONALLY DETOX YOUR HOUSE

Now that you've pared down and cleared the clutter using the Create Space for Your Future exercise, you may realize there are still things that weigh you down, beyond the purely physical dimensions of your home environment. This is because people attach sentiments to objects, even if unconsciously. The time of your life, the emotion, the aspiration—they are all energetically tagged onto what you own or buy. Without you knowing it, your house becomes a storeroom of different energies, some of which work for you, and others that work against you. Inspired by Ingrid Fetell Lee's TED talk, this exercise will help you detox your home of the emotions you no longer want to keep around. Here, you will reflect on prompts linked to two different emotions that have built up in your house. In the space provided, you can journal about objects related to each emotion, or any particular place in your house where these objects tend to accumulate.

Shame is a feeling that gets in the way of joy, self-acceptance, and living well. When you feel ashamed of yourself, you feel bad about the person that you are. Objects in your house that store shame could include, for example, things that you excitedly brought home, keen to use for self-improvement, but then never touched again. Some items that may store shame are:

- Exercising or dieting gear you don't enjoy or haven't used in a long time.
- Clothes, skincare products, and cosmetics you don't like but wear to look "acceptable" or to please someone else. They could be things you don't fit into anymore but keep for "someday."
- Books, art, and music that don't reflect you or your tastes, but you believe you "should" like.
- Unfinished hobbies and projects that you've lost interest in or haven't made the time for that therefore make you feel bad about yourself for not completing.

Stuckedness is about the projects you started but ended up putting on hold because circumstances changed. Whenever you are faced with these constant reminders of your life being stuck in limbo—that space between what was and what could have been—it's easy to feel deflated. Items that carry a feeling of stuckedness might include:

- The things you save for a future version of yourself that could really be used right now. For example, beautiful clothes or precious heirlooms, or that expensive candle or fancy china.
- Clothes still in their bags and/or with tags attached.
- Art that hasn't been framed or displayed and is either propped against a wall or in storage.
- Items you don't want and have been meaning to return or that you've outgrown.
- Suitcases and boxes left unpacked because you thought this space would be temporary.

Here are things in my home that I feel shame about:

_____

_____

_____

_____

_____

_____

_____

_____

_____

_____

Here are things in my home that bring out feelings of stuckedness:

_____

_____

_____

_____

_____

_____

_____

_____

_____

_____

When you're faced with daily reminders of shame and stuckedness, it is difficult to feel good about yourself and the life you're creating. These toxic feelings sap away the vital energy you need to enjoy the present and move confidently toward the future.

This exercise invites you to discover what you have piled up, and then thoughtfully choose what emotions, like shame and stuckedness, you no longer want to store in your house. As you go about this, you may find you feel emotional saying goodbye to some of them, and yet you may also experience a sense of relief. Know that there is strength in letting go and in making space for the type of person you want to become.

Connecting with What Matters

Here's how I felt doing this exercise:

_____

_____

_____

_____

_____

_____

_____

_____

_____

_____

Here's what surprised me, reflecting about where shame and stuckedness are stored in my home:

_____

_____

_____

_____

Here are the emotions I choose to give to these spaces instead of shame and stuckedness:

_____

_____

_____

_____

In the space provided, reflect on the following questions, and jot down the ideas that come to mind.

1. With the things that bring shame, what can you enjoy in their place?

For instance, what books or art could you swap them for?

_____

_____

_____

_____

2. How could you realign your goals with actions or objects you enjoy?

For instance, instead of obsessing over your skin daily in magnifying mirrors, you could use beautifully scented skincare. Or you could finally get rid of the treadmill you've been using as a clothes rack and commit to taking a long walk outside every day.

_____

_____

_____

3. How can you better use the objects you want to keep?

For instance, frame the paintings. Or decide when you'll use the fancy dinner plates: Are there rules you can create around when to pull them out? Are there occasions you can invent for them?

_____

_____

_____

_____

4. What's your plan to unpack the boxes and suitcases?

_____

_____

_____

_____

5. For all the stuff you no longer want, create a plan to either discard it or find a better home for it:

_____

_____

_____

_____

6. As you watch your space clear and experience the negative emotions release with the clutter, reflect on how good that feels: Use this feeling to motivate you to keep things this way.

_____

_____

_____

_____

SET UP YOUR ENVIRONMENT
FOR SUCCESS

What habits have you been unsuccessful at sticking to—that you know would make the difference in living a life focused on the things that matter? You know the fundamentals—eat, sleep, move, and drink healthily. They seem so simple, but it's a case of easier said than done. And then there's the bigger personal and professional goals you have; they seem straightforward enough in your head. Except you either never start or don't finish them. Chances are, you've criticized yourself and felt you might never reach your goals. Here's the deal: Slow or stalled progress is not the big moral failure that you believe it to be. Otherwise, there wouldn't be a seemingly endless stream of books, workshops, and courses focused on building habits and reaching goals. Keeping up with new habits and seeing your goals through can be hard. But there are things you can do to make it easier, including setting up your environment for success.

For each habit you want to cultivate, this exercise first invites you to consider the following five questions. In particular, you will want to focus on what gets in the way, so that you can create a solution that you can't ignore.

What's the habit I want to grow?	Why do I want to do this?	What gets in the way?
_____	_____	_____
_____	_____	_____
_____	_____	_____
_____	_____	_____

How can I make the action of that habit impossible to ignore?

_____

_____

How can I reward myself?

_____

_____

The following are examples of positive behaviors, common obstacles to taking action, and suggested solutions to get around the challenges. You can adapt these to your own habits.

HABIT: Taking supplements, drinking water	
Obstacle:	Solution:
You forget because out of sight, out of mind.	Put the pills where they are unmissable, such as by your bathroom sink; put bottles of water all around your house.

HABIT: Exercising	
Obstacles:	Solutions:
Obstacle 1: You talk yourself out of it in the morning. **Obstacle 2:** When you come home to get your gear, you sit on the sofa and watch TV.	**Solution 1:** Lay out your exercise clothes by your bed, where you will see them. **Solution 2:** Hang your gym bag by the door, so you don't even step fully inside your house to grab it.

HABIT: Working consistently on your project rather than procrastinating	
Obstacles:	Solutions:
Obstacle 1: You are physically uncomfortable. **Obstacle 2:** You are tired and uninspired.	**Solution 1:** Get a better chair or seat cushion. **Solution 2:** Schedule this project during your most productive and inspired hour; diffuse refreshing scents like peppermint or lime to jolt your brain.

Understanding Why This Matters

When you continuously criticize yourself for being unsuccessful at cultivating a habit, the fear center in your brain is activated. This is not only hazardous for your confidence in your ability to get things done; it's also bad for your health. Instead of locating the problem within yourself, which means you are calling yourself lazy or incapable, see if external factors are really what's to blame. Has your environment been set up to sufficiently support you?

The water that flows when you turn on the tap and the lights that shine through your room at the flick of a switch do not just happen by magic. They work because of certain systems. In this exercise, you have learned to create your own systems so your habits eventually seem to run by themselves. To get somewhere, you first need to examine what *stops* you from getting there. From the ergonomics of a comfortable chair to a scent that pushes the primitive parts of your brain into action, these simple systems help you form good habits, because you cannot ignore their effects. Similarly, placing things within sight—where they are impossible to miss—means you can trick your brain into thinking that you have no choice but to do them. Over time, these actions start running on autopilot, becoming a habit.

Connecting with What Matters

Here's how I see my ability to get things done differently after doing this exercise:

_____

_____

_____

_____

_____

_____

Here's what surprised me about the science of forming habits:

_____

_____

_____

_____

_____

_____

First, identify the three or four life areas in which you'd like to cultivate new habits. Ideally, you will start by creating an action plan for two habits in each of these areas, so you can get lots of practice in finding creative solutions. However, you will only take action on one habit in each area at a time, so you don't get overwhelmed.

1. _____   3. _____

2. _____   4. _____

Sometimes, people are unhappy about how these habit-helping objects do not fit with the aesthetic or neatness of their home. This is understandable—some of us prefer for things to match or not stand out. But there are ways to get around this. For example, if you're creating a habit around taking vitamin supplements, you could organize them on a tray that matches your decor, or put them in matching glass bottles with printed labels. Keep creating solutions; do not talk yourself out of growing the habit!

You can assess your progress by measuring (1) how often you stuck to the habit, (2) how quickly you integrated the habit into your life, and (3) what you could do differently to maximize success. Record your progress in the chart provided. Once a habit has become largely automatic, you can start focusing on the next one.

HABIT:		
How often I stuck to the habit:	How quickly I integrated the habit into my life:	What could I do differently to maximize success:

Remember to reward yourself as motivation to continue with the good work.

CREATE A WORRY CORNER AND WORRY TIME

Everyone worries—it's part of being human. Worrying is one way you experience anxiety, and anxiety evolved to signal to humans when to retreat in order to conserve resources and figure out how to best move forward. Unfortunately, sometimes anxiety gets the better of you, and worrying becomes your default mode. So, instead of simply retreating to make a plan, the *act* of worrying takes over your head, energy, and time—leaving very little room to focus on what matters. And because you worry in all areas of your house, simply being at home triggers more worrying.

This exercise will help you to reclaim control over worrying and compartmentalize the act of worrying within a designated part of your house. In this way, both your time and your space will feel lighter.

1. **Location:**

Designate a spot in your house to worry. It should be quiet and out of the way. Some people choose a particular armchair or a corner of a room. From now on, this will be the *only* spot you will engage in worrying.

Here's where my Worry Corner will be:

_____

_____

2. **Time:**

Designate a set time on your calendar every day. If you typically worry for six hours a day, you may decide to start with a two-hour Worry Time. Schedule it in, and set an alarm. This will be the time when you have free rein to worry as much as you want. You may decide to worry at different times every day, or on weekdays versus weekends.

Here's when my Worry Time will be:

_____

_____

3. A Safe Spot:

Choose a Safe Spot where you'll mentally file your worries. It could be a filing cabinet or a jewel-toned velvet box. It doesn't matter, as long as you feel reassured that your worries are safe and sound.

Here's my Safe Spot:

_____

_____

Now, here's what you will do every time a worry pops into your head outside of your Worry Time:

- Acknowledge your worry as a neutral fact, like the stars in the sky. You can say, "I am worried about [subject]."
- Next, jot down what the headline for the worry would be if it were a news article. Keep it concise, a maximum of five words.
- Take three deep breaths and mentally visualize filing your worries in your Safe Spot.
- Go back to what you were doing, knowing that you'll tackle your worries during Worry Time.

Here's what to do during your Worry Time:

- Prep yourself with a comforting drink like a warm cup of tea or coffee.
- Head to your Worry Corner.
- Set a timer.
- Worry all you want!

Understanding Why This Matters

There is a difference between worrying and planning: Worrying amplifies fears, while planning solves problems. However, some people find the act of worrying to be comfortable because it's familiar. You're so used to doing it, and may even wonder who you are if you're not worried. With this exercise, you can still worry, but you'll keep it compartmentalized within a given time and space.

When you worry everywhere throughout your house, the energy of anxiety lingers in every space. This causes your environment itself to trigger more worries—a needless vicious cycle. Gifting yourself with a Worry Corner means you can do more purposeful or fun things in the other parts of your house, which will encourage more of these positive states of mind.

Designating a Worry Corner and Worry Time helps you be in control of how you spend your time and energy.

Connecting with What Matters

This is how I feel when I acknowledge my worries outside of Worry Time:

_____

_____

_____

_____

_____

Here's how I feel after Worry Time:

_____

_____

_____

_____

_____

Taking Action on What Matters

Most people end up needing only about half the time they designated for Worry Time. Or you may find that you prefer a different time slot.

1. **Assess**

Use the following prompts to observe how your Worry Time goes for a week, then review what changes you may want to make.

I have:

☐ enough
☐ too little
☐ too much

Worry Time.

I am:

☐ happy
☐ unhappy

with my Worry Time time slot.

Here's what I will do differently going forward:

_____

_____

_____

2. Refocus

Next, decide what you'll do with the time you've freed up. You can create categories for the different activities, such as "by myself," "with friends," and "with family"; or "learning" and "fun." This will give you an organized list to choose from.

Category 1:   Category 2:   Category 3:

_____   _____   _____

_____   _____   _____

_____   _____   _____

_____   _____   _____

_____   _____   _____

Write down what you will do in other parts of your house. You could designate different types of activities for certain areas.

Area 1:   Area 2:   Area 3:

_____   _____   _____

_____   _____   _____

_____   _____   _____

_____   _____   _____

_____   _____   _____

3. Reflect

Consider how your sense of control over worrying is evolving over the weeks of using a Worry Corner and Worry Time, and write down your reflections here.

This is how much control I had over worrying before:	After one week, this is what's different:	After one month, this is what's different:
_____	_____	_____
_____	_____	_____
_____	_____	_____
_____	_____	_____
_____	_____	_____

Finally, write down how your house makes you feel as time passes.

Here's how I felt about my house before:	After one week, this is what's different:	After one month, this is what's different:
_____	_____	_____
_____	_____	_____
_____	_____	_____
_____	_____	_____
_____	_____	_____

DESIGN BETTER MORNINGS AND NIGHTS

You start and end your days in your bedroom. Lack of space or being glued to your smartphone means the bedroom can be an unpeaceful place where it's difficult to sleep. Whether it's insomnia, waking up in the middle of the night, or feeling poorly rested in the morning, unhealthy quality and quantity of sleep is a problem for many people. Designing better mornings and nights that help you feel energized and engaged in what matters in your daily life starts with getting rid of the obstacles to bad sleep and instead optimizing your bedroom environment.

In this exercise, you'll consider the following bedroom elements:

- Bed: For sleep and sexual activities only. Check the comfort levels of your mattress and pillows.
- Tech: Your phone should be far away from your bed—do not touch it just before sleeping or first thing when you wake up. Avoid having a TV in the room. Use a physical alarm clock.
- Temperature: Set your personally ideal temperature using a fan, air conditioner, heater, and/or blankets.
- Color: Decorate the room with soothing, warm colors like forest green or taupe.
- Light: Use low lights, lamps, and candles, not harsh overhead lighting. Blackout curtains may be helpful.
- Security: Feel safe in your room by using a door lock and other privacy measures.
- Sound: Keep the room as quiet as possible; white noise machines and ear plugs can help.
- Smell: Diffuse or spray soothing scents like lavender, sandalwood, and jasmine.

Understanding Why This Matters

Sleep is non-negotiable. It is the cornerstone of your physical and mental fitness, affecting everything from work performance to relationships. Adequate rest involves having both a sufficient amount and a good quality of sleep.

Connecting with What Matters

Here's what struck me most about my bedroom in doing this exercise:

_____

_____

_____

_____

_____

_____

_____

Here's what I now understand as obstacles to good sleep:

_____

_____

_____

_____

_____ .

_____

_____

Taking Action on What Matters

1. What needs to change?

First, evaluate things that could be changed in your bedroom that will have the greatest impact on your sleep.

Here are the three most pressing changes:

1. _____

2. _____

3. _____

2. Set a deadline:

Next, set a deadline and plan to implement these changes (think about time, practicality, and budget).

I will implement these changes by: _____ .

3. Assess challenges:

Are there any challenges you may face? How can you get around them? You may ask for help or do research.

Here are potential challenges and their solutions:

_____

_____

_____

_____

_____

_____

4. Assess activities moving out of the bedroom:

Finally, think about activities, like entertainment or work, that you're moving out of the bedroom, and where you could create alternative spaces for them.

Here is a list of activities I will move out of the bedroom:

_____

_____

_____

_____

_____

_____

CREATE YOUR (DIGITAL) HOME SWEET HOME

Are you calm when you think of all of your devices and online storage? Or do your shoulders seize up while you convince yourself that everyone has five thousand unread emails? Whether or not you know it, digital clutter can be just as anxiety-provoking as physical clutter. So in your journey toward determining what matters, getting organized digitally should also be a top priority.

1. **Set a goal.**

How organized would you like to be? Typical areas that need organizing include your emails (actual emails and newsletters), bookmarks (in your browsers and social media apps), contacts lists, photos, and computer folders. Would having a lot of email subfolders work, or would a few be enough?

These are the areas that need organizing:

_____

_____

_____

_____

2. **Draw out the organizational levels you'll need for these areas.**

What *rules* would your digital "home" benefit from? These could include immediately deleting every email that doesn't matter, only subscribing to the few newsletters that matter, going through the photos you've taken at the end of every day or week, and archiving every email once you've read and responded to it.

These are three basic rules I'll set for myself:

1. _____

2. _____

3. _____

Understanding Why This Matters

A messy, cluttered digital home depletes your energy, even if you think it's no big deal. The longer this goes on, the greater the loss of control, because the clutter starts to feel like it takes on a life of its own as it piles up. Things are hard to search for, and wading through the mess is overwhelming. In short, it gets in the way of focusing on the things that actually matter.

Connecting with What Matters

This is the part of my digital home I'd benefit most from organizing:

_____

_____

_____

_____

_____

Here's exactly how I'll benefit from organizing:

_____

_____

_____

_____

_____

Taking Action on What Matters

Prioritize what you'd like to organize, book a time in the calendar for each to-do, and do them. You may also look up the easiest ways to get organized, to help kick-start your own organization efforts.

To stay motivated, reflect on these questions:

- Before starting this exercise, how did the thought of your digital home make you feel?
- How did the thought of getting organized make you feel?
- And how did you feel after getting more digitally organized?

PLAY TOURIST IN YOUR HOME CITY

Have you explored your home city the way you explore other places? Most people are likely to answer no. The yearning and curiosity that you have when abroad may be significantly muted or even absent when you think about the area where you live. The thing is, your home city is an extension of your home, and a good relationship with it colors and enriches your everyday life. When you see your city as somewhere exciting or with places you've yet to explore, you have feelings of both comfort and novelty...instead of boredom.

1. **What do you enjoy while traveling?**

     What do you do when abroad? Seek out particular things, like art, music, or theater? Prioritize food or outdoor activities?

Here's what I gravitate toward when traveling:

_____

_____

_____

_____

2. **Why do you enjoy these things?**

     What drives these preferences? It could be because you prioritize aesthetics or love history. Or maybe because they make your go-to travel partner happy, and that matters most to you.

This is what drives what I do when traveling:

_____

_____

_____

_____

3. **Look at where you live through a different lens:**

Imagine what it would be like to be a tourist in the place where you live, and experience it like you experience other places.

Here's how I see playing tourist in my home city:

_____

_____

_____

Here's what I would do differently being a tourist at home versus while traveling:

_____

_____

_____

_____

If I were to show a foreigner around my home city, here's what I'd do, and why:

_____

_____

_____

Understanding Why This Matters

It is human nature to take what's familiar for granted. You may tie your home city to the everyday routine that includes your obligations, boring errands, and work. And in your head, going abroad is the grand escape from these things. While that's a great reward and way to recharge, you can also create amazing moments in your home city by giving yourself things to look forward to every day or week. You can find things that matter to your most engaged self right outside your door.

Connecting with What Matters

Here's what I've realized about my attitude toward my home city in doing this exercise:

_____

_____

_____

_____

_____

_____

_____

_____

_____

_____

Here's how I want to give my home city the same thoughtfulness or reverence I give to places when I'm traveling:

_____

_____

_____

_____

_____

_____

_____

_____

_____

Taking Action on What Matters

The following are things you can do to find the amazing in your everyday life:

- Research your city online and create a list of what you can do based on your priorities identified previously in this exercise.
- Get into the same actions and mindsets as when traveling. Do you go on a road trip? Take photos?
- Join a walking tour to learn something new.
- Play tourist with someone who's got great energy you admire.
- Document your experiences online by combining them with other interests like photography or writing.

RITUALIZING SUCCESS

You maximize success by getting clear on the journey, which is what you'll do in this exercise. First, you'll identify rewards, so your brain gets that feel-good dopamine boost whenever you do what you set out to do. Next, you'll figure out what stands in your way, so you're not surprised, but rather prepared to tackle these obstacles head-on. Then, you'll set mini-milestones so you can check in with yourself to ensure you're on track and practicing your new skills and habits without needlessly second-guessing yourself.

Rewarding Myself

I'll reward myself when I reach these mini-milestones:

_____

_____

_____

_____

Here's how I'll reward myself: (include both small and big rewards)

_____

_____

_____

_____

Identifying Obstacles

These are the factors that might make this journey more difficult:

_____

_____

_____

_____

Here's what I can do to get around these challenges:

_____

_____

_____

_____

These are the beliefs that stand in my way:	Here's what I can do to get around these beliefs:
_____	_____
_____	_____
_____	_____
_____	_____
_____	_____

Checking In

Here's how long I'll dedicate to discovering what matters to me right now: _____

I will check in with myself every_____ .

Putting It All Together

Now that you've filled out the previous sections, integrate them here. Then, set these review dates in your calendar:

Date:	Goal:
Date:	Milestone:
Date:	Milestone:
Date:	Milestone:
Where I am now:	

CHAPTER 5

Discovering What Matters in Your Career

Most people plan their lives around their work, squeezing everything else around it as an afterthought. Their relationships, health, and home life fight for scraps of time and attention. You may also have found that your career has taken on a life of its own, evolving since you first entered the workforce. Chances are, you're a different person now with other priorities. This means that the old ways of thinking or acting may not work for you any longer.

In this chapter, you'll first pause and consider which career season you are in now, who you are in the world of work, and what you want from this world. From here, you'll make yourself and your priorities the solar system around which your career revolves (versus the other way around). Maybe this will mean reinventing yourself career-wise. Or maybe your standards for perfection that are really dragging you down need to change. Then you'll start working on how to create your new reality, with exercises that teach you helpful skills like disagreeing and agreeing productively, giving and taking support, harnessing motivation, and creating more time and energy for what matters.

SETTING INTENTIONS AND GOALS

To support your success in the exercises that follow, answer these questions about your intentions and goals for this chapter.

I want to feel_____ about my career.

As I discover what matters in my career, I want to become the type of person who_____

_____ .

This is what I want to accomplish from discovering what matters in my career:

These are the mini-milestones I'm breaking this larger goal into:

_____	_____
_____	_____
_____	_____
_____	_____
_____	_____
_____	_____
_____	_____
_____	_____
_____	_____
_____	_____
_____	_____
_____	_____
_____	_____
_____	_____

DETERMINE WHAT CAREER SEASON YOU ARE IN

If you constantly feel that dread every Sunday—what psychologists call the "Sunday Scaries"—or that sense of weariness on Mondays, then you might want to think about doing something differently in your career. Many people see work as suffering—something they hope to get over as soon as possible. The benefits that come with their career are a trade-off, the price to pay for making ends meet or living a comfortable lifestyle. But what if you could enjoy the work you do? That doesn't simply mean having fun or being passionately positive 100 percent of the time. It could mean feeling like you are making an impact on someone or growing as a professional. This way, you don't simply go through the motions, watching the clock and counting down to your weekends.

In this exercise, you'll examine how you've evolved during the course of your work life, and if you want anything to be different going forward. This reflection is based on your overall career or your current role:

The career/role I'm examining is_____ .

The time length I'm considering here is _____ .

Who were you before?

This is who I was at the beginning of this career/role:

_____

_____

_____

_____

This is what I wanted then:

_____

_____

_____

_____

What did you give up to be here?

Consider the sacrifices and trade-offs you've made, related to time and your mental fitness, for example.

_____

_____

Who are you now?

Consider how you've evolved.

This is who I am now:

_____

_____

_____

This is what I...

Love about my job:	Tolerate about my job:	Hate about my job:
_____	_____	_____
_____	_____	_____
_____	_____	_____
_____	_____	_____
_____	_____	_____
_____	_____	_____

Consider which of the following you have right now, and whether they line up with what matters to you.

☐ A sense of purpose

☐ Loving what you do

☐ Autonomy

☐ Recognition (e.g., praise, more responsibility)

☐ Pay and other monetary benefits

☐ Non-monetary benefits (e.g., vacation, parental leave, remote working)

☐ Room to grow (e.g., advancement options, mentorship)

☐ Healthy work environments (e.g., no toxic colleagues)

☐ A sense of teamwork

These are the things I value in a career now:

_____

_____

_____

_____

_____

_____

Having done this reflection, read bestselling author Ramit Sethi's three categories of career seasons and decide where you are:

- Growth Season: When you prioritize earning and learning and are willing to invest the time to get where you want to be.
- Lifestyle Season: When you want to prioritize your time and energy outside of work, such as spending time with loved ones, growing a side business, or simply resting more.
- Reinvention Season: When you want to join another industry, take on a completely different role, or reinvent who you are as a professional.

The career season I'm in is: _____.

Understanding Why This Matters

Time flies—you evolve more than you know, as a person *and* in terms of what you want. Earlier in your career, your priorities may have been different. Some things like flexibility and time may have felt like luxuries, and you were willing to sacrifice sleep or tolerate bad behavior. As you grow in your skills and responsibilities, and life exposes you to different experiences, you learn what you like and dislike in your career. But rather than adapting your professional life around your changing priorities, you may settle, persisting at what makes you unhappy or dissatisfied.

The thing is, career often forms the core of a person's identity. You also spend many of your waking hours on work. And then work-related matters may continue to rule your mind after the workday is done. Your career therefore significantly impacts your mental and physical health.

Giving yourself space to examine what matters in your career—based on your experiences so far—will help you become more thoughtful about your work life and understand what you really want. You can then make the changes that will get you to where you want to be.

Connecting with What Matters

Here's how I've changed professionally since the start of my career/role:

_____

_____

_____

_____

_____

_____

_____

_____

_____

_____

_____

_____

_____

Here's what I've realized about my career through this exercise:

_____

_____

_____

_____

_____

Here's how much control I feel over the next chapter of my career:

_____

_____

_____

_____

_____

Here are some prompts to help you chart a plan forward, based on your career season:

Growth

- What's my goal for Growth Season?
- What do I need to do?
- What will I prioritize my time and energy for?
- What's the trade-off?
- How long will this season be?
- How can I keep myself motivated when the going gets tough?

Lifestyle

- What do I really want?
- Why haven't I asked for it?
- What stories do I tell myself that stop me from asking for what I want?
- How can I do less of what I merely tolerate or actively dislike?
- How can I ask for what I want (with evidence for why I deserve it)?

Reinvention

- Why do I want this?
- Do I know what I want next?
- What do I need to do more (e.g., research, network)?
- How can I create continuity between now and the future, so I can leverage my experience to get me there?
- Do I have an exit strategy from my current career?
- What do I need to create this exit strategy?
- How can I build my safety blanket to cushion me as I transition?
- What's my timeline for this season?

NAME YOUR CRAFT

You have about four hours of peak productive time every day—if you have optimum energy levels. When you force unrealistic standards onto every area of your life, expecting yourself to be 100 percent productive and successful in everything all of the time, you overtax yourself. Over time, you pay a steep price that puts your sleep, health, and energy in debt. If you want to be excellent at work, then you need to negotiate your priorities. This exercise will help you to figure out which areas of your career you'd like excellence in, and you'll learn the importance of negotiating "good enough" standards in other parts.

These are the things within my career that chew most of my energy:

_____

_____

_____

_____

Being *artisanal* means devoting yourself to a certain craft, putting in the time, focus, and practice needed to perfect it. For you, this could be leadership or mentoring skills, or writing, or any area you feel particularly drawn to. Maybe your lifestyle or identity revolves around it. It could be something practical to your professional role, or what you're proud of.

This is what I'd like to be artisanal in:

_____

_____

_____

_____

_____

_____

_____

This is what being artisanal looks like to me:

_____

_____

_____

_____

_____

_____

_____

These are the "good enough" standards I'll commit to in the other parts of
my work life, so I have more energy for my craft:

_____

_____

_____

_____

Understanding Why This Matters

There comes a point when pushing for the best costs you disproportion-
ately more time, energy, and peace. When you scramble to meet impossible standards in everything, the focus you could have devoted to what
matters is diluted. This is unproductive, because everything suffers, down to
the people you were trying to please. And you lose your zest for what truly
matters, the part of your work that has the potential to truly inspire you.

Connecting with What Matters

Here's what I learned from this exercise about the standards I have:	Here's what I learned from this exercise about what I truly want to be excellent at:
_____	_____
_____	_____
_____	_____
_____	_____
_____	_____
_____	_____
_____	_____

Taking Action on What Matters

1. Take steps to hone your craft

This is the one key action I'll take to pursue excellence in my chosen craft:

_____

_____

_____

_____

2. Set realistic expectations
There will be times when you'll still want to push for unrealistic standards in the other parts of your work life.

This is how I'll remind myself to follow the "good enough" standards:

_____

_____

_____

_____

3. Assess performance

As I've freed up time and energy, this is what I've noticed about my performance, energy levels, and zest in my chosen craft:

_____

_____

_____

_____

GO FURTHER BY PARTNERING WITH OTHERS

Some people see partnering with others as a waste of time and productivity. This perspective can be valid, as there are times when working on a team does lead to distractions, confusion, or frustration. But, if done effectively, working together can allow you to harness different strengths and ideas to get the best outcomes, and create a strong and healthy workplace culture. This exercise invites you to consider how you can become part of a culture where people support and elevate each other, and by doing so, go further toward what matters together.

1.   How do you receive support?

     First, consider how easy it is for you to *receive* support from the following people. It may be asking for support or taking it when offered. You could think in terms of asking for tangible help such as outsourcing, collaborating, or exchanging ideas, or seeking feedback or advice.

From people at a similar level:	From those at a higher level:	From those at a lower level:
_____	_____	_____
_____	_____	_____
_____	_____	_____
_____	_____	_____

What's your overall relationship with receiving support? When you think about this, what patterns do you notice?

_____

_____

_____

Are there any areas where you could do with extra support? If so, what's stopped you from getting it?

_____

_____

_____

How would you benefit from receiving more support?

_____

_____

_____

2. How do you provide support?
Next, consider how easy it is for you to *provide* support to the following people. It may be offering support unprompted or giving it when asked.

From people at a similar level:	From those at a higher level:	From those at a lower level:
_____	_____	_____
_____	_____	_____
_____	_____	_____
_____	_____	_____

What's your overall relationship with giving support? What patterns do you notice?

_____

_____

_____

Are there any areas where you could do with providing extra support? If so, what's stopped you from doing that?

_____

_____

_____

How would you benefit from providing more support?

_____

_____

_____

3. Do you have a support system?

Now consider if you have people you trust to turn to. They could be mentors in similar or different careers, peers, or others with wisdom to offer.

If your answer is yes:

What does this support look like? How does it serve you? Would you like this support to be any different?

If your answer is no:

Who would you ideally like in your circle of trust? Why do they belong there?

_____

_____

_____

_____

_____

_____

_____

_____

How do you generally respond when someone trustworthy offers constructive advice? Think in terms of both solicited and unsolicited advice.

_____

_____

_____

_____

Understanding Why This Matters

Healthy work cultures allow everyone to shine. People share ideas and experiences, and uplift each other. There's a team spirit where everyone works toward the same bigger goals.

Of course, cultures are made up of individuals. University of Pennsylvania organizational psychologist Adam Grant studied people who give support more than they receive it, people who take more, and people who give and take at an even level. He found that both the best and worst performers are givers, while takers are midlevel performers. More importantly, the best performers are the givers who give support in a way that suits their strengths, and still look out for their own interests. In other words, it's about having boundaries rather than dropping everything you can to help someone else. And it's about honoring your own needs and agenda.

When you break this down across three different levels of support with the different people above, below, and parallel to you in your career, you have a bird's-eye view of how things are and what you can tweak to create a more ideal situation for everyone.

Connecting with What Matters

Here's what I've learned from this exercise about my personal balance between receiving and giving support:

_____

_____

_____

_____

Here's the extent to which I'm happy about how I work with others, and what I'd like to change:

_____

_____

_____

_____

Taking Action on What Matters

1. Brainstorm meaningful support

Consider how you can give support in meaningful ways that energize you. These are likely to be things you're already good at doing, and that take less than five minutes. Or you can plan a bigger project such as setting aside an hour every month to mentor your juniors.

_____

_____

_____

2. Brainstorm growth

Another way you can grow with someone else is through coaching, where you identify areas you'd like to grow or habits you'd like to break. Top performers in every field seek out coaching, and work with coaches in ways that suit their lifestyle, personality, and goals.

These are some areas where coaching might be helpful for me:

_____

_____

_____

3. Create a circle of mentors

Work on putting together your own circle of mentors. You can simply start by reaching out, introducing yourself, and being helpful to them.

My circle of mentors includes:

_____

_____

_____

4. Assess your workplace culture and how it relates to support

If you're finding it difficult or even impossible to give and receive support, then you might want to consider the culture of accountability where you work. Certain workplace cultures take responsibility and look for solutions. Others are about pushing blame and staying in a victim mindset. Or you could be around people who like to hog credit and take favors.

My workplace culture for support looks like:

_____

_____

_____

FREE UP CHUNKS OF PRECIOUS TIME

When you rush from one task to another, you may think you're getting things done as efficiently as possible. But when you engage in projects, meetings, and activities back-to-back without breaks, they feel like one massive chunk of responsibilities. It then becomes harder to tease out individual components of your day to reflect on or strategize about. Over time, this is the recipe for burnout.

This exercise shows you how to make space between the different parts of your day, so you have more clarity around the things you do—and whether they are truly in line with what matters to you—and more energy to get them done. You'll spend a little time to buy yourself a lot of time and sanity. To do this, you'll need to schedule ten-minute windows of time before and after each activity you engage in.

Ten Minutes Before Task

Use these questions to guide your task in the ten-minute window *before* the task:

This is what I'd like to get out of this task:

_____

_____

_____

_____

In order for this to happen, I will focus on:

_____

_____

_____

_____

This is how I'd like to feel after this task is over:

_____

_____

_____

Any last-minute inspiration:

_____

_____

_____

Ten Minutes after Task

Use these questions to reflect on your task in the ten-minute window *after* you're done:

If I were to summarize what just happened in a few headlines, they'd be:

_____

_____

_____

_____

Going forward, this is what I plan to do as part of my task list:

_____

_____

_____

_____

This is my biggest takeaway:

_____

_____

_____

Any other thoughts:

_____

_____

_____

Understanding Why This Matters

Ten-minute windows allow you to reflect with more intention, instead of going through the motions with less clarity and mental energy, which creates more messes for you to clean up. Ten-minute windows will translate to less time working overall.

Connecting with What Matters

Here's how I felt before trying
ten-minute windows:

_____

_____

_____

_____

_____

_____

_____

_____

_____

_____

_____

_____

Here's the difference I've
observed after practicing this
exercise:

_____

_____

_____

_____

_____

_____

_____

_____

_____

_____

_____

Taking Action on What Matters

First, commit to taking ten-minute windows between tasks. Consider what life would look like if you were burned out. You can also pair this with the short breathing exercise in Reset Your Brain in Chapter 2 to help transition from one task to another with a clean slate.

SCHEDULE WHEN TO PRESS "PAUSE" AND "PLAY"

If you were to consider your work life as a video, are you on continuous "play" mode, or do you hit "pause" enough? This goes beyond designated work hours or longer breaks like weekends and vacations. A *pause* is a deliberate rest to recharge. The problem is that the idea of "I'll sleep when I'm dead" is associated with strength and success. But that attitude is a surefire way toward mental and physical health crises. If this nonstop loop is something that resonates with you, think about whether you could get through ennui and tiredness, reclaim your old passion, *and* get to the next level, simply by pressing "pause" more.

This exercise invites you to examine the relationship between intense work and resting, and gives you the chance to schedule in a better balance of *pause* and *play*. Use the "pause" button to rest up so that when you hit "play" you are coming into the things that matter with more energy, focus, and excitement.

1. **What is your work momentum?**

    First, consider the intensity of your work momentum. For some people, it varies across the day or week. For instance, they may have some busy hours or days. For others, they may have busy seasons, such as during the holidays or the end of the financial year.

Here's what my work momentum is like:

_____

_____

_____

_____

Here's how I feel about this momentum:

_____

_____

_____

_____

These are the changes I'd love to make to my momentum, if possible:

_____

_____

_____

_____

2. **How do you recharge?**

Next, consider when you recharge or power down. This may be after work, on weekends, or during days off. Also examine to what extent you are truly resting.

These are the times I have scheduled in for rest:

_____

_____

_____

_____

This is the extent to which I'm truly resting:

_____

_____

_____

_____

Here's what interrupts my rest time:

_____

_____

_____

Here's what I'd like to change about this:

_____

_____

_____

3. **What does your attitude toward rest look like?**

Now consider your attitude toward resting—anything from "rest is weak" to "rest is essential"—and where that attitude comes from. For instance, you might personally appreciate rest but come from a culture that frowns on it.

This is what I think about resting and why:

_____

_____

_____

_____

_____

Because it's easy to forget to rest, it's important to integrate downtime into your schedule. One simple way to do this is to follow the moon's phases, since you can simply take your cues from the sky:

- New moon: When a new lunar month starts, set goals, intentions, and actions.
- Waxing phase: As the moon grows larger, work hard and smart.
- Full moon: While the moon is full, celebrate your accomplishments—and rest a little!
- Waning phase: As the moon grows smaller, gradually power down and reflect on your work.
- Dark moon: The last few days before the new moon, rest more and spend more time with yourself.

Understanding Why This Matters

Even if you've witnessed firsthand just how revitalizing rest can be, you may shun it because of the social or cultural values you subscribe to. Adam Grant, an organizational psychologist and TED speaker, distinguishes between unhealthy and healthy cultures by noting that unhealthy cultures see rest as "taking your foot off the gas pedal. You don't stop until you've pushed yourself to the brink of exhaustion." In healthy cultures, rest is a fuel—regular breaks recharge you as you go after what matters, and you avoid burnout.

When you rest, the "default mode network" in your brain is activated. This makes you likelier to create breakthroughs, because your brain is able to consider previously unrelated concepts or ideas. Not to mention, the things you do when you rest can be material for your creativity.

Following the lunar cycle is an easy way to build both rest and momentum in your work, because it is in harmony with nature. There's scientific evidence that humans, like most animals, are affected by the moon. Different ancient calendars, from the Chinese to the Hindu and Jewish, are based on moon phases.

This is my attitude toward resting:

_____

_____

_____

_____

_____

Here's what I'll do differently going forward:

_____

_____

_____

_____

_____

Taking Action on What Matters

You can integrate a lunar calendar into your existing calendar. Start by searching online for "phases of the moon."

The following are ways you may use the lunar cycle to rest or charge forward at work. Read through, and write your plan for each aspect in the provided space.

1. **Personal and professional development**

You might time new projects during the new moon, and use the waxing phase to attack a large part of the work or to work closely with a coach. During the waning phase, you might reflect on what's worked, and what could be done differently. And then you may draw your game plan for the new month ahead.

_____

_____

_____

_____

_____

2. House/office decor

You might use the full moon to deep clean and declutter your space, and the new moon to style the space differently.

_____

_____

_____

_____

_____

3. Social

You might network more actively during the waxing phase, and spend more time on yourself and your most important relationships during the waning phase.

_____

_____

_____

_____

_____

4. Body and mind

You could time the waning moon with massages, stretching, and eating healthier, and schedule in reflective therapy. You might then use the waxing moon for more intensive goal-oriented workouts and coaching.

_____

_____

_____

_____

_____

LEARN TO DISAGREE AND AGREE PRODUCTIVELY

Some people agree with everyone; others disagree with everyone. Although disagreeing gets a bad rap, it's not always a bad thing. When people always agree, there's no space to be creative or express what matters to them as individuals. Maybe no one dares to rock the boat or consider other possibilities. When people can't play well together, there's tension and it's difficult to get things done. This might be because they don't know how to disagree productively, or they're being objectionable on purpose.

This exercise will teach you to agree and disagree better, so that your conversations are more productive.

1. Reflect on a time you disagreed with someone:

    Think back to a time when both parties *disagreed*, and the outcome was unfavorable for everyone.

Did you listen and consider the other person's stance? If so, was it just to argue against it, or to find some point of similarity?

_____

_____

_____

Were you rushing to build up your ideas? Was this because you felt you weren't being listened to? Were you worried that you'd forget your main points? Or is this your default in a disagreement?

_____

_____

_____

How did the other person act?

_____

_____

_____

2. **Reflect on a time when you** agreed **with someone outwardly but felt differently inside:**

What was going on?

_____

_____

_____

Did you feel pressured to agree, or feel there wasn't enough time to compose your argument?

_____

_____

_____

Or did you feel it was not worth expressing your views about the situation? If so, was it because the other person always gets their way, or because it was a minor situation?

_____

_____

_____

Understanding Why This Matters

Learning to disagree and agree better is a win-win-win for you, the other party, and the relationship or outcome. It's essential for effective communication. First, you learn to listen to what they are saying, and also observe what's *not* being said. This involves being present—not stuck in your own head. Second, you learn to find solutions that take everyone forward.

Connecting with What Matters

Generally, I am more...   ☐ agreeable   ☐ disagreeable

These are the internal factors
that make me this way:

_____

_____

_____

_____

_____

_____

_____

_____

_____

These are the external factors
that have shaped me in this way:

_____

_____

_____

_____

_____

_____

_____

_____

_____

Taking Action on What Matters

When everyone is disagreeing, curl your toes so you're brought into the moment and forced to listen deeply. Then find a point of similarity, offering how you agree and suggest how you'd like to take things forward for everyone's benefit. Use "Yes, and" instead of "Yes, but" to enhance cooperation. Finally, always ask, "What do you think?" to invite conversation.

If it's difficult to disagree, jot down your main thoughts in a few headlines. Start the conversation with "I'd like to make a suggestion." Keep it short and to the point, so everyone can process it easily. And again, always ask, "What do you think?" so everyone's involved.

HARNESS MOTIVATION

Making changes in order to get what matters to you can feel terrifying. In your comfort zone, things are certain. Even if your current actions aren't exactly the healthiest, you have some inkling of where they will lead you. But with change comes the risk of uncertainty, which naturally stirs up anxiety. What if you fail? And then, what if you succeed? Would you necessarily like that? One key thing that keeps people going through the ups and downs of change is motivation. When motivation knocks, you ride its wave. While that means you can't necessarily rely on it all the time, you can learn how to harness it from within.

In this exercise, you'll compare the costs with the benefits of a change you're about to make. Seeing the benefits can be just the motivation you need to push forward.

This is my goal: _____

Here's why I'm doing this:

_____

_____

_____

What does my life look like right now?

_____

_____

_____

What changes need to be made?

To create change in pursuit of your goal, you can take any number of actions. Consider only the main changes that will lead to meaningful outcomes.

The main changes I'll make:

_____

_____

_____

What are the costs of these changes?

Be specific about what embarking on this change will cost you. For most people, this includes the resources invested or doubts about the change or the future.

Here's what it will cost me to change:

_____

_____

_____

Are there benefits of not making changes?

Next, consider the advantages of keeping things the way they are. For most people, the advantages range from how it's easier to not apply any effort, to how they have ways to temporarily cope with the things they're unhappy about. Know that this question can come with discomfort, because the answers can be difficult to tease out and admit. Therefore, acknowledge any discomfort you have, and answer as honestly as you can, knowing that you'll grow from this exercise.

Here are the benefits of not changing:

_____

_____

_____

What are the benefits of changes?

Consider how your life would be different if you made these changes. How would you feel waking up in the morning? Would you look any different? What would your general state of mind be? Also, how would you see yourself as a person?

Here are the benefits of changing:

_____

_____

_____

Finally, consider what life would be like in a year's time if you continued doing the same things. What would make you feel uncomfortable about that future? How would you see yourself?

Here's what it will cost me to *not* change:

_____

_____

_____

Understanding Why This Matters

For any change to happen successfully, you need a plan...and fear about the future should you continue the status quo.

Anxiety—about the future and making a change outside of your comfort zone—is a black hole for your time and energy. When you're clear about the consequences of maintaining the situation as is, you realize that the issue goes beyond how things never change. As you let things continue the way that they are, your confidence in your ability to make future changes in that area of life will shrink more and more—this is what psychologists call "learned helplessness." In this exercise, you learned to channel that anxiety about the future and change effectively, and train yourself to move toward change while paying attention to realistic limits.

This exercise also teaches you about "secondary gain": the benefits of the status quo. People sometimes enjoy their temporary coping mechanisms and need an excuse for them, or they secretly enjoy the attention they get when they talk about their misery. Getting honest about this helps you to understand your motivation for not wanting to change, so you can start to truly let go of these obstacles, and learn to channel your motivation toward productive change.

Connecting with What Matters

Here's how I felt doing this exercise:

_____

_____

Here's what I've realized about why I sometimes don't want to change things:

_____

_____

Here's what I've learned about myself when it comes to motivation:

_____

_____

Taking Action on What Matters

As you go about creating a life filled with what matters, there will be times you'll want to give in to your old habits. And sometimes you might. That's part of being human: Do not take it personally or sabotage yourself further. What matters most is you're able to recommit to your action plan.

One way of helping yourself to stay committed is to consider the two "future selves" you are facing, depending on what you do. One is the ideal future self: the fruit of the changes you make. The other is the undesirable future self: the consequence of not changing. So, when choosing what you are going to do, let this question guide you: "Does this take me closer to my ideal future self, or my undesirable future self?"

The more you do this, and the more specific you allow yourself to get when picturing both futures, the more you'll activate the part of your brain that allows you to see your present and your future selves as the same person. Why is this good? People who see both selves as one and the same are more likely to do things that are good for their future, *and* more likely to delay gratification, holding out for the bigger rewards that come with time and effort.

FUEL YOUR CAREER WITH YOUR DARK ENERGY

Like everyone else, you've got something in your life that's made you dissatisfied or angry, or there's something you're not proud of. You may not know what to do with it, and work very hard to suppress or deny it. When times are tougher—like in the wake of a crisis—this "dark energy" can resurface, and you may feel like it's taking over. The good news is, you don't have to engage in a Dr. Jekyll and Mr. Hyde type of struggle. You can use your dark side to fuel your career in a way that benefits everyone.

In this exercise, you will reflect on your own brand of dark energy. People have aspects of themselves or emotions that they feel aren't "acceptable" and that society discourages. These include anger and rage, entitlement, a cruel streak, or enjoying playing the victim. As you do this exercise, you might judge yourself or feel uncomfortable. In this case, it can help to imagine you're doing a medical scan of your personality and character: Put yourself in that scientific frame of mind to get more objective and answer the questions as honestly as you can.

Here are the parts of myself that I don't like:

_____

_____

_____

_____

Think about some event in your life, such as during your childhood, when this dark energy showed up.

Where did the dark energy come from?

_____

_____

_____

_____

Now think about the things that have happened inside you or around you over the years that have reinforced that dark energy.

What has made the dark energy stronger over time?

_____

_____

_____

_____

When I entertain my dark energy, here's how it benefits me:

_____

_____

_____

_____

Here are the things that trigger my dark energy:
   (e.g., something someone says)

_____

_____

_____

_____

If I unleashed my dark energy, here's what would happen:
   (e.g., long-term consequences)

_____

_____

_____

_____

Here's how I know the dark energy is coming up:
   (e.g., overwhelming thoughts or certain physical sensations)

_____

_____

_____

_____

How can my dark energy be channeled into my work?
   (e.g., laser-focus on a project, or work hard to prove someone wrong)

_____

_____

_____

_____

Bestselling author Robert Greene has spoken extensively about how, instead of pretending that dark energy doesn't exist, people can learn to understand it and channel it into a positive force. For example, legendary basketball player Michael Jordan channeled his anger about being cut from his high school varsity team into winning championships.

When you can channel your dark side effectively into the things that matter to you in your work and beyond, the other parts of your life also run more smoothly, because you are not suppressing parts of yourself (or burning up energy in that process). In fact, people will perceive you as more authentic and be drawn to you.

Your dark energy can be especially helpful during a crisis, giving you that extra boost to push through the shock, doubt, and more.

Connecting with What Matters

Here's what I have realized about my dark energy and where it comes from:

_____

_____

_____

_____

_____

_____

_____

_____

While doing this exercise, here's how I felt facing my dark energy:

_____

_____

_____

_____

_____

_____

_____

_____

Taking Action on What Matters

Now that you've explored your dark energy, here's a game plan to work through the different aspects and use them to your advantage.

Every time you feel a trigger, acknowledge it to yourself, and do the breathing exercise in Reset Your Brain in Chapter 2. This will help you integrate your dark energy rather than suppress it, and get your higher brain onboard to make wiser decisions.

Next, explore this dark energy even more deeply—maybe aspects are linked, or there are parts you are still not aware of. You can explore this with a professional, with the explicit aim of using this self-discovery to become a more integrated person, and use this dark energy as a source of motivation.

Instead of judging yourself, practice having empathy for your younger self, knowing that you did the best you could in that situation. Whenever this dark energy emerges, you could ask yourself, "How could I be the champion my younger self never had?"

Finally, the obstacle to your integrated self is whenever you play too nice, agreeing with others or allowing them to trample on your boundaries. Get clear about these situations and make an action plan for what you will do differently.

Moving forward, when dark energy emerges, I will:

_____

_____

_____

_____

TURN IMPOSTOR SYNDROME INTO A BENEFIT

Almost everyone suffers from some version of impostor syndrome, especially in their career. Common beliefs include "I'm a fraud" and "someone is gonna realize I'm not what they think I am." While this is normal, it's also exhausting, and as is, does not benefit anyone. All that energy you waste focusing on the negative voice in your head could be better used to build mental strength and resilience, and be more engaged with the people around you.

In this exercise, you'll get clear on that tiresome monkey on your back, so you can change impostor syndrome into something a lot more productive.

1. **Reflect on where in your career you believe you aren't good enough.**

In what ways do you feel like you are a fraud in your job?

_____

_____

_____

_____

_____

_____

_____

What's the evidence for that?

_____

_____

_____

_____

_____

_____

How often do you feel this way?

_____

_____

_____

_____

_____

_____

_____

On a scale of 1–10 (10 being the strongest), how strong is your sense of impostor syndrome? (circle one of the following numbers)

1 2 3 4 5 6 7 8 9 10

What tends to trigger it?

_____

_____

_____

_____

How does this make you feel? Where do you experience these feelings in your body?

_____

_____

_____

_____

When did you start feeling like a fraud? Consider what was going on in your life at the time.

_____

_____

_____

_____

When you feel this way, what do you do to make that feeling of self-doubt go away? Reflect on how these actions help or cost you in the long run.

_____

_____

_____

_____

When you think of the term "impostor syndrome," what are the beliefs about yourself that automatically come to mind?

_____

_____

_____

_____

What do you really think will happen should you continue to be this impostor you think you are?

_____

_____

_____

_____

For instance, think about the ways you are living smaller than you should, or the opportunities you bypass.

_____

_____

_____

_____

2. Are your feelings of impostor syndrome based on a previous version of yourself?

Impostor syndrome happens because people base their perceived competence levels on some younger and less mature version of themselves. Naturally, their younger selves were less sophisticated and skilled, and may have done what their current selves judge to be incompetent things. When you consider your fears about being "found out" from that angle, of course you worry.

Who were you before?

What is the version of yourself around which *you* are defining your competence? How old is this self? What did they do that you're not proud of? And what was going on in the background of their lives?

_____

_____

_____

_____

Who are you now, and how have you grown?

_____

_____

_____

_____

Understanding Why This Matters

Put simply, impostor syndrome is when your confidence lags behind your competence, almost as though you are operating based on two different versions of yourself. You pick up skills along the way. And as time speeds ahead, you haven't paused to take stock of how you've really grown. Unbeknownst to you, this person you think hasn't got the skills or maturity is only a previous version of you. This exercise updates the operating system of your head, letting your confidence catch up with your competence.

Impostor syndrome isn't always a bad thing. It shows that you know that there are parts of you that could benefit from growing, and that you have skills to hone. And every time you feel a new version of it pop up, use that as an opportunity to explore how far you've come and what you would like to do going forward to keep improving and getting closer to what matters to you.

Connecting with What Matters

Here's what I've learned from this exercise about what my competence is really like:

_____

_____

_____

_____

_____

_____

_____

_____

If I could turn back time, here's what I would do differently:

_____

_____

_____

_____

_____

_____

_____

_____

Taking Action on What Matters

Reflect on the extent to which your current self does *not* qualify to be called an impostor:

_____

_____

_____

_____

_____

_____

_____

_____

_____

_____

What wisdom can you teach your younger self?

_____

_____

_____

_____

_____

What expired beliefs about yourself do you choose to let go of?

_____

_____

_____

_____

_____

Do you celebrate yourself and your accomplishments enough? What can you do differently going forward?

_____

_____

_____

_____

_____

In which areas do you realistically need more growth or improvement, and how would it benefit you?

_____

_____

_____

_____

_____

How do you feel about needing this growth or improvement?

For some people, this might trigger insecurity or further impostor syndrome. Others may get upset about being a late bloomer.

_____

_____

_____

_____

How can you use your strengths to help you grow or improve?

_____

_____

_____

_____

Being humble teaches you to stay grounded and to keep growing. Where do you think you need more humility?

_____

_____

_____

_____

As philosopher Alain de Botton said, if you don't feel embarrassed by the younger version of yourself, then you haven't grown.

RITUALIZING SUCCESS

You maximize success by getting clear on the journey, which is what you'll do in this exercise. First, you'll identify rewards, so your brain gets that feel-good dopamine boost whenever you do what you set out to do. Next, you'll figure out what stands in your way, so you're not surprised, but rather prepared to tackle these obstacles head-on. Then, you'll set mini-milestones so you can check in with yourself to ensure you're on track and practicing your new skills and habits without needlessly second-guessing yourself.

Rewarding Myself

I'll reward myself when I reach these mini-milestones:

_____

_____

_____

_____

Here's how I'll reward myself: (include both small and big rewards)

_____

_____

_____

_____

Identifying Obstacles

These are the factors that might make this journey more difficult:

_____

_____

_____

_____

Here's what I can do to get around these challenges:

_____

_____

_____

_____

These are the beliefs that stand in my way:

_____

_____

_____

_____

Here's what I can do to get around these beliefs:

_____

_____

_____

_____

Checking In

Here's how long I'll dedicate to discovering what matters to me right now: _____

I will check in with myself every _____ .

Putting It All Together

Now that you've filled out the previous sections, integrate them here. Then, set these review dates in your calendar:

Date:	Goal:
Date:	Milestone:
Date:	Milestone:
Date:	Milestone:
Where I am now:	

CHAPTER 6

Discovering What Matters in Your Community

Being part of a community matters. The evidence is unanimous: Loneliness literally kills, while great relationships help you grow and enrich your life. Beyond personal relationships, people define themselves as members of certain groups. Your collective self can also become a gateway to more one-on-one relationships.

In this chapter, you will figure out what community means to you and the types of communities you'd like to be part of, based on the energy and time you have and what matters to you. If the thought both excites you and scares you, then you can benefit from the exercise that trains your brain to connect successfully. You'll also build skills like making personal introductions, finding easy ways to build community, and spearheading action within groups—with and without technology. Finally, you'll inject warmth in your everyday community: the people around you.

SETTING INTENTIONS AND GOALS

To support your success in the exercises that follow, answer these questions about your intentions and goals for this chapter.

I want to feel _____ about my community.

As I discover what matters in my community, I want to become the type of person who _____

_____ .

This is what I want to accomplish from discovering what matters in my community:	These are the mini-milestones I'm breaking this larger goal into:
_____	_____
_____	_____
_____	_____
_____	_____
_____	_____
_____	_____
_____	_____
_____	_____
_____	_____
_____	_____
_____	_____
_____	_____
_____	_____
_____	_____

IDENTIFY WHAT COMMUNITY MEANS TO YOU

Most people are already part of communities of sorts. Maybe it's a group that you're automatically associated with, through your job role or where you live. Or it could be something you've inherited. Your communities also evolve over time, because the existing ones change, or you become involved with others. In this exercise, you'll reflect on what community truly means to you.

When you consider the word "community," what comes to mind?

_____

_____

What does your community look like now?

Consider the size, if it's online or offline, what you do together, and how you feel after interacting.

_____

_____

_____

List up to three of the primary communities you're part of.

1. _____

2. _____

3. _____

What's the common force that drew the members of your community together?

What do you talk about? What do you like about it? What's lacking?

_____

_____

_____

What do you like most about your current community?

_____

_____

_____

_____

_____

What do you admire about people who are part of strong communities?

_____

_____

_____

_____

Is there anything you miss about your old community? If yes, what is it?

_____

_____

_____

_____

_____

How much time and energy do you realistically have to be part of a community?

_____

_____

_____

_____

Is this past community still relevant to your current self? If so, how can you re-create some of that in your current life?

_____

_____

_____

_____

_____

What are the biggest obstacles to being part of a community? (e.g., being unsure where to start, or unable to drive to an event location)

_____

_____

_____

_____

Understanding Why This Matters

You have more power in shaping the groups you're part of than you might think. But sometimes it takes a crisis to make you reevaluate what's still relevant or set new priorities you'd now like to focus on. Often, when life changes, people romanticize the past. Upon further reflection, you may realize that the things you say you miss about an old community may be pure nostalgia, or its benefits are inflated in your mind.

Connecting with What Matters

Here's how satisfied I am about my current involvement in communities:

_____

_____

_____

_____

_____

_____

Here's what I've learned about these communities I'm part of:

_____

_____

_____

_____

_____

_____

Taking Action on What Matters

Going forward, consider how much involvement you'd like to have with a certain community. For instance, some people like activities that are more like "parallel play," like reading together but not actively talking all the time. Others want a community where everyone is active on a chat group between meetings.

Also, think about how your community ties in with multiple goals or impacts different areas of your life. Often, when these are more intertwined, you are likelier to commit to them.

FIGURE OUT WHAT YOU WANT
FROM COMMUNITY

Now that you've identified what community means to you and how much time and energy you can give, you can narrow down your focus so you know exactly where to start looking. A good first step is to consider how you'd like to personally benefit from having a community, because this motivates you to get going. This exercise organizes communities into categories to help keep you from feeling overwhelmed by all the possibilities. You will brainstorm as many relevant options as possible within each category.

The following are four broad categories of communities. Journal your ideas—be as specific and creative as you can.

1. Common interest

You may want to be part of a community around a *common interest*. This could be around a broad culture like a country, a theme like food or art, or an activity like a book club.

_____

_____

_____

_____

2. Accountability

Some people want *accountability* around a certain goal. For instance, you may find it difficult to wake up to hike alone, and therefore want to do it with others. Or you are an entrepreneur who'd like to share the journey with your peers who understand your experiences.

_____

_____

_____

_____

3. Support

Others would appreciate *support*. This could be due to similar backgrounds like being a parent, or what's going on in your life such as a mental health group.

_____

_____

_____

_____

4. Give back

Some people want to be part of a community to *give back* to society. Consider where you could volunteer your expertise and the causes you are passionate about.

_____

_____

_____

_____

Understanding Why This Matters

This is an exercise in creativity and power, so you demonstrate to yourself that you always have options and can actively choose your path in life. Engaging in a common interest might translate to more fun or learning, while accountability makes you likelier to do something and hit the goal. Having support means you know you're not alone. Last, giving back helps people to feel purposeful.

These are the types of community I'm most interested in:

_____

_____

_____

_____

_____

_____

_____

_____

These are the types that will be the easiest for me to try out:

_____

_____

_____

_____

_____

_____

_____

_____

Taking Action on What Matters

Start by testing out different groups according to the communities you've identified. Some groups will be a better fit than others; the more you try, the more you will find what resonates with you. Adopt a mindset of curiosity. Otherwise, you might get discouraged, because it's easy to feel dejected or tired when something doesn't work as well as expected. Consider what made you like some communities, and what made you dislike others.

After experimenting for a certain time period, set a date to review and make a list of communities you'd like to commit to.

WIRE YOUR BRAIN TO CONNECT SUCCESSFULLY

Sometimes, before you can connect in meaningful ways, you need to figure out what stands in your way. As the late expert in loneliness John Cacioppo found, sometimes disconnection isn't simply about lack of social skills or support. When your brain gets used to being lonely, it literally turns on itself and against you. The effects of loneliness build, and you become more isolated. This exercise is designed to help you if you find it difficult to make new connections, especially in the wake of a crisis when your confidence may have already taken a hit.

Consider your responses to each of the following statements and jot down your thoughts in the space provided. For instance, the extent to which you agree with each statement, when you're likely to feel or think that way, and the consequences. Think about these in relation to meeting new people, even if you already have some close relationships.

I'm suspicious of most (new) people.

_____

_____

_____

_____

I'm too eager to please people I've just met.

_____

_____

_____

_____

I'm too eager to trust (new) people.

_____

_____

_____

_____

I feel judged when I talk to people.

_____

_____

_____

_____

I'm often lost in my head, judging myself for not acting or being good enough, when I'm around other people.

_____
_____
_____
_____

I have a tendency to either withhold information about myself or tell people way too many personal details.

_____
_____
_____
_____

I am out of practice in interacting with new people and don't know how to start.

_____
_____
_____
_____

I worry about my performance before, during, and long after an interaction.

_____
_____
_____
_____

I think it's easier to simply not interact with others.

_____
_____
_____
_____

I've always been terrible at connecting.

_____
_____
_____
_____

After what feels like a flimsy interaction, I feel deflated and give up.

_____
_____
_____
_____

Now think about the last time you talked to someone new. Or, observe yourself when you next meet someone, in order to consider the extent to which you agree with these statements:

- ☐ My posture is hunched.
- ☐ My arms/legs are crossed tightly.
- ☐ My shoulders feel tight.
- ☐ My heart is beating too fast.
- ☐ My hands/legs are sweaty and/or shaky.

Here's the kind of person you believe most (new) people judge you to be:

_____

_____

_____

Many people think that being self-conscious and analyzing their performance when interacting with others will keep them from making mistakes or embarrassing themselves.

Some people believe that after their midtwenties, it's impossible to make new connections; others believe that practical problems like anxiety or their obligations and jobs stand in the way.

Why do you think it's hard to make new connections?

_____

_____

_____

Understanding Why This Matters

The impact of obligations, failures, and tiredness builds up as we grow older, and it becomes easier to say no to things that might require some time but would nevertheless be good for us in the long run. Instead, we find it easier to say yes to the quick fix of unhealthy habits that might feel like a temporary salve. Often your world shrinks without you knowing it, and unless you purposefully spend the time to make new connections or deepen existing relationships, you get lonelier. You start buying into ideas that you cannot connect or are bad at connecting, and your body confirms it with symptoms of anxiety like a fast heart rate and a hunched posture.

If you agreed to at least half of the statements in this exercise, chances are that loneliness has taken over. Teasing out the thoughts, experiences, and feelings behind it is your first step to wiring yourself to connect successfully in the future.

Most who seem natural at connecting weren't born that way. They simply make themselves available to having genuine social interactions that are appropriate to the context, while also having strong boundaries that ensure they are respected.

Connecting with What Matters

Here's how I felt doing this exercise:

_____
_____
_____
_____
_____
_____
_____
_____
_____
_____

These mindsets stand in the way of me connecting with others:

_____
_____
_____
_____

These are the connection-building skills I need to develop:

_____
_____
_____
_____

First, if you're finding it hard to quiet your anxious thoughts during an interaction, do the breathing exercise in Reset Your Brain in Chapter 2 to keep you focused. Being an engaged listener will benefit you a lot more than trying to sound clever or witty. Here are more tips for successful interactions:

- If you think most people are intimidating or even scary, then your brain may be reading facial cues wrong. You may want to engage a coach or therapist to help you retrain your brain to better read others.
- Keep your posture open, standing or sitting straight, to teach your brain that you're in control of the situation.
- Use the Identify Who You'll Say What To exercise in Chapter 3 to help you figure out what's appropriate to say to whom.
- Brainstorm about low-risk environments within which you might be able to make new connections, such as your work or volunteering. You can use insights from the Tap In to Existing Resources to Build Community exercise later in this chapter.
- Go into this practice with the mindset that you're collecting data on what you're good at when it comes to connecting with others, what you need improvements in, and the people you're more compatible with—everything is feedback, not something to feel bad about.
- Keep reviewing your progress and refining your action plan.
- Expect some successes, and celebrate them.

LEARN HOW AND WHERE TO INTRODUCE YOURSELF

Once you hit your late twenties, the opportunities for making new friends seem to dwindle. And true, when you're younger, you are more often in environments where you are around potential friends, which makes the forming of relationships easier. However, if you practice making friends, then the process can become as natural as brushing your teeth, no matter your age. Of course, it's easy to feel deflated because you will inevitably meet some people you don't gel with. Or you may feel overwhelmed by crowds. The secret is to address the challenge in a way that excites you and that fits your personality.

This can be broken down into *how* and *where* you introduce yourself. The *how* is about gathering information about yourself, which you can selectively use in your introductions. The *where* is about the contexts in which you introduce yourself and the way you go about it.

1. Reflect on who you are:
   Read the following prompts and write down your answers.

You spend most of your days doing:

_____

_____

_____

Here's how you'd describe yourself as a person:

_____

_____

_____

The top three things you're proudest of are:

_____

_____

_____

The top three things/people that have made the deepest impact on you, and why:

1. _____
   _____
2. _____
   _____
3. _____
   _____

Something interesting about you that few people know about:

_____
_____
_____
_____
_____
_____

What you'd love to do if you could simply wave a magic wand:

_____
_____
_____
_____
_____
_____

If you were to choose three to five adjectives to describe yourself, they'd be:

- _____
- _____
- _____
- _____
- _____

2. **Ask people you trust to reflect on who you are:**

Now ask five people you trust the following questions, and jot down notes here. You could use this script to get things rolling: "I'm doing this exercise for personal/professional development, and have to ask some people I trust some questions about me. Would you be cool with sparing ten minutes?" You could do this during a call or meeting, or ask for answers in writing.

- What do you like most about our relationship?
- How would you describe me to a stranger?
- What do you think I'm great at?
- What surprises you most about me?

Take notes on their answers here:

_____

_____

_____

_____

_____

Based on this information, use the following space to uncover the main themes about who you are and what makes you unique.

_____

_____

_____

_____

3. **Pick the choice that best completes the statement for you:**

I recharge best...
- ☐ by myself
- ☐ in one-on-one interactions
- ☐ in large crowds
- ☐ in all of these ways

4. **Finally, consider what information about yourself is appropriate to share for different contexts.**

These could range from professional networking to a local tour to talking to a stranger reading a book you love.

Understanding Why This Matters

Crafting your personalized introduction gives people a glimpse into the unique person that you are. This invites the other person into a more meaningful conversation with you, especially if you happen to share similar interests or backgrounds. If a detail you've shared piques their curiosity, it will deepen the interaction.

Figuring out how you recharge will teach you the environments to seek out. Introverts recharge best by themselves or one-on-on, so they do better in more intimate settings such as smaller events like a Meetup group or a book club. In larger events, introverts should aim to strike deep conversations with one or two people. Extroverts recharge in large groups—the more the evening goes on, the more incandescent they become. They do well in larger crowds and by interacting with more people. As for the ambiverts, who are equally recharged by themselves and in crowds, they can mix both types of interactions.

Tailoring your introduction to the environment also means you learn to flexibly express the best parts of yourself that are the most relevant to a given environment, so you shine in any given situation. You don't need to feel compelled to tell everyone everything. In museums, you admire art pieces because there's loads of white space, and the pieces are thoughtfully curated. Think of yourself, and the way you introduce yourself, in that same way.

Connecting with What Matters

Here's what I've learned about myself through this exercise:

_____

_____

_____

_____

Here's how I've been underselling myself in social settings:

_____

_____

_____

_____

Doing this exercise, I felt:

_____

_____

_____

_____

1. Craft your introduction.

Here are ways to start:

- "Hi, I'm [your name], and I'm here because of a long-standing interest in [subject] since [time]. [One sentence about how this started/what struck you in particular]."
- You could also connect this introduction to your job or background and make it specific. For instance, "psychologist for overachieving leaders" gives someone else way more insight than "psychologist."
- "Hello, I'm [your name]. I'm really looking forward to [event] because [reason based on the story of your life or what you'd love to do]."

_____

_____

_____

_____

_____

2. Practice your introduction.

Next, you'll practice your introduction by visualizing or role-playing with people. Or, practice in a low-stakes, low-stress environment. This could be at some informal gathering like a luncheon hosted by a friend, so you won't feel bad even if you are not as polished as you'd hoped.

3. Assess mindset during interactions.

Last, adopt the mindset that this is a numbers game. You will meet some people you'll love talking to, and some you have no chemistry with. Take every encounter you have as an opportunity to get prime intel about what you're good at, what you enjoy, and what you'd like to get better at.

TAP IN TO EXISTING RESOURCES TO BUILD COMMUNITY

The idea of building community can sound daunting, especially if you have little experience or feel out of touch with others. Because of that, many people put it off. The problem is that forming new connections gets harder the more you delay, because your belief that you are bad at it only grows with time. What you may be overlooking is an already existing resource, namely yourself and your social circle. This exercise helps you to tap in to your current networks to discover low-effort and low-risk ways to go about building community.

The following are examples of how you might build community through your existing circle(s):

- If you already know people from different areas of your life who are keen to do an activity or engage in a cause, round them up.
- Ask a few friends to bring one friend each to a gathering.
- Reconnect with someone you've lost touch with.
- Ask someone you know for a referral or warm introduction into a certain group.
- Outsource the responsibility to a friend who likes to plan things or who's been saying, "You should really be a part of [event/activity/group]" for a long time.

And here are easy ways to build community on your own:

- Do an activity you've always wanted to try, to enable following up with your new acquaintances. For instance, a class, a walking tour, or communal gardening.
- Spearhead a project through your job or your business.
- Think of places where you're already somewhat connected, such as in a club or a class.
- Go one step further and volunteer to help.
- Join a Meetup group or try an app for making new friends, like Bumble BFF.

Understanding Why This Matters

Doing something out of your comfort zone triggers resistance, especially for social activities. This is even more significant for introverts and people with social anxiety, or when a crisis has hit and your self-image has been impacted. Moreover, people are innately afraid of being rejected—you are wired to perceive social rejection as physical pain. This exercise is about identifying the low-hanging fruit you can pick to help you take your first steps toward confidently building a sense of community.

Connecting with What Matters

Before I started this exercise, here's how the idea of building community made me feel:

_____

_____

_____

_____

Here's what feels different after doing this exercise:

_____

_____

_____

_____

Taking Action on What Matters

Choose one activity you'll undertake on your own, and another you'll participate in through an existing social circle. You could write a script in advance to make the request. Or use the exercise Learn How and Where to Introduce Yourself earlier in this chapter to craft your introduction.

If you're comfortable, you could even post on social media. Make it interesting and specific, with a call to action. For instance: "Looking to put together a monthly book club for crime fiction fans. Message me."

Adopt the mindset that not everyone is going to become your bestie— you will mesh with some people better than others.

HOST YOUR OWN EVENT

Steve Jobs once said, "People don't know what they want until you show it to them." Sometimes it's up to you to invent what hasn't been invented yet (at least where you live). If your ideal community is nowhere to be found, or you have a vision of combining different aspects of communities that already exist, then you may benefit from hosting your own event and building your community around that. Consider the following prompts and write your inspiration in the space provided.

What's your vision for this community?

_____

_____

_____

_____

_____

What would you like to get out of this community?

_____

_____

_____

_____

_____

What makes this community different?

For instance, a specific target demographic like "under-thirties" or "entrepreneurs."

_____

_____

_____

_____

Is it a sit-down event involving food and/or drinks? Something more active like playing a sport? Does it involve the same or different locations or communities?

_____

_____

_____

_____

This could be the conversation topic, food, or dress code.

_____

_____

_____

Consider the venues or technology that's already out there.

_____

_____

_____

_____

_____

Can you outsource it?

_____

_____

_____

There are times when you have to step up, take things into your own hands, and lead. This is a lot easier if you love hosting or are particularly passionate about the type of community you are creating.

This exercise helps you to hammer out the logistics and determine if you'd realistically require some extra support; some people do best when each member of a founding team (or pair) plays to their strengths.

Connecting with What Matters

Doing this exercise, I was surprised to learn this about myself:

This is what excites me most about hosting:

Taking Action on What Matters

1. Create an action plan

Armed with this information, you can begin drawing up an action plan. Elements to keep in mind include:

- The style and content of invitations
- Where and how to reach your target community (see the Tap In to Existing Resources to Build Community exercise earlier in this chapter)
- Any required bookings for venues
- Getting clear on who contributes what

2. Reflect on the event

At the end of the event, reflect on how it went. Consider these questions:

- What did you enjoy most about this experience?
- What would you have preferred to be different?
- What surprised you the most?
- Would you do this again? Why?
- How would you describe this event to a friend?

KINDLE SOME WARMTH IN YOUR EVERYDAY COMMUNITY

Everybody has ideas of what it means to be part of the community around them. This could be neighbors bringing food, everyone on an entire street gathering for an annual party, or fellow runners saying "hi" as they pass each other. It could also be about the kindness—when a security guard in your building looks out for your safety, or a next-door neighbor offers an umbrella because it may rain—that shows you people care.

In this exercise, you'll consider how you can take control of injecting some warmth and human connection into everyday life.

When you think of people being part of their wider community, these are the images that come to mind:

_____

_____

_____

These are the activities where you're likely to meet people who are doing the same things, and say "hi" to spread the kindness:

_____

_____

_____

Here's where the inspiration from the previous prompt comes from:
(e.g., stories, movies, places)

_____

_____

_____

_____

Here are the everyday situations in your life that could do with a little warmth, like smiles or casual conversations:

_____

_____

_____

_____

Some ideas to guide you:

- Smile and greet the people who make your life easier, like cleaners and security guards, or those doing similar activities, like fellow hikers or others with kids and/or dogs in the park.
- Thank your bus or rideshare driver.
- Pay for the coffee order for the person in line behind you; buy a meal for someone who's homeless.
- Introduce yourself to your neighbors with food.
- Casually chat with your local barista or food server.

Understanding Why This Matters

Community isn't simply the people you hang out with or the groups you are a member of. Little slices of connection and warmth can help everyone feel valued, even if this isn't the norm in your culture. A smile is free!

Connecting with What Matters

Doing this exercise, here's what I learned about myself:

_____

_____

_____

_____

_____

_____

_____

_____

Here's how I see "community" differently now:

_____

_____

_____

_____

_____

_____

_____

_____

Taking Action on What Matters

The actions suggested in this exercise may be out of your comfort zone, so notice if you have any resistance and how you may talk yourself out of it.

Reflect on these things here:

_____

_____

_____

_____

In those cases where you feel uncomfortable, ask yourself, "What's the worst that could happen?"

Reflect on the worst-case scenario here:

_____

_____

_____

_____

You might benefit from observing someone you know who is warm with everyone—you'll likely notice that they are sincere but not intense.

Jot down your thoughts on this person:

_____

_____

_____

_____

Last, you can use the script in the Learn How and Where to Introduce Yourself exercise earlier in this chapter to strike up a friendship with someone you share a warm moment with.

USE TECHNOLOGY TO CONNECT MORE DEEPLY

Sharing recommendations and thoughts in your *Insta*-stories and on *Facebook*, exchanging opinions about what's going on in the world, posting a callout for people to engage in an activity: Technology can be the glue for people to feel like part of a bigger community. But often, that time spent taking photos and posting them in real time can mean people aren't actually interacting. Instead, most people are focused on simply putting their voice out there. In this exercise, you'll learn how to use technology more thoughtfully to build a deeper sense of community.

There are many reasons why technology may be important for *you* in connecting with the community. Maybe you're new to the area, are a third-culture kid (meaning you were raised in a culture outside of your parents'), or you spend a lot of time online to begin with: Connecting digitally may be part of your work or a generational norm.

So, why is using technology to plug in important to you?

_____

_____

_____

_____

What are the different specific ways in which you use technology to interact with your community?

_____

_____

_____

_____

What are the ways in which digital connection may harm you or your community?

It's important to consider the possible cons of digital tools, like feeling more isolated by only posting without actually connecting to others, so you can prevent or fix these issues.

_____

_____

_____

_____

_____

There are three main types of online communities you may like to join or build, especially if it's not practical or possible to meet in person.

1. Discussion/ interest groups

   What *discussion/ interest groups* are you curious about?

   _____

   _____

   _____

   _____

   _____

   _____

   _____

2. Support groups

   What *support groups* are you curious about?

   _____

   _____

   _____

   _____

   _____

   _____

   _____

3. Action groups

   What *action groups* are you curious about?

   _____

   _____

   _____

   _____

   _____

   _____

   _____

If you're keen and have the time and energy, you may even decide to volunteer your services in these groups to cement your commitment and relationships.

What can you contribute to these groups?

_____

_____

_____

_____

Understanding Why This Matters

More and more, technology is becoming a vital part of the lives of many people. And while some warn about it being harmful, it is ultimately a tool that is as useful or destructive as you make it. And part of what makes you a product of advanced human evolution is the ability to use the tools available.

Connecting with What Matters

Here's what I've learned from this exercise about the role of technology in building community:

_____

_____

_____

_____

_____

_____

_____

_____

_____

_____

Here's how I felt doing this exercise:

_____

_____

_____

_____

_____

_____

_____

_____

_____

_____

_____

Taking Action on What Matters

1. Identify how you can connect thoughtfully using technology

What is one thing you can do to use technology to connect with others more thoughtfully, and how will this impact you?

_____

_____

_____

_____

2. **Connect with people to ensure effective use of technology**

Have a conversation with the people with whom your digital connections may be less than effective right now, so everybody benefits from technology going forward. Include these details:

- How the digital tools serve everyone.
- Where maintaining the digital connections gets a bit tricky, and why.
- How encountering challenges with the technology makes you feel.
- A suggested tweak to how you use digital tools to connect.
- Ask them "What do you think?" to invite conversation and create a way forward that benefits everyone.
- Thank them whenever they engage with discussions on this topic.

3. **Identify online groups you're keen on joining:**

_____

_____

_____

_____

4. **Finally, follow up individually with people you resonate with, so you cultivate deeper personal and collective ties.**

RITUALIZING SUCCESS

You maximize success by getting clear on the journey, which is what you'll do in this exercise. First, you'll identify rewards, so your brain gets that feel-good dopamine boost whenever you do what you set out to do. Next, you'll figure out what stands in your way, so you're not surprised, but rather prepared to tackle these obstacles head-on. Then, you'll set mini-milestones so you can check in with yourself to ensure you're on track and practicing your new skills and habits without needlessly second-guessing yourself.

Rewarding Myself

I'll reward myself when I reach these mini-milestones:

_____
_____
_____
_____

Here's how I'll reward myself:
(include both small and big rewards)

_____
_____
_____
_____

Identifying Obstacles

These are the factors that might make this journey more difficult:

_____
_____
_____
_____

Here's what I can do to get around these challenges:

_____
_____
_____
_____

These are the beliefs that stand in my way:

_____

_____

_____

_____

_____

Here's what I can do to get around these beliefs:

_____

_____

_____

_____

_____

Checking In

Here's how long I'll dedicate to discovering what matters to me right now: _____

I will check in with myself every_____ .

Putting It All Together

Now that you've filled out the previous sections, integrate them here. Then, set these review dates in your calendar:

Date:	Goal:
Date:	Milestone:
Date:	Milestone:
Date:	Milestone:
Where I am now:	

CHAPTER 7

Discovering What Matters Through Adventure (or Experiences)

The most meaningful and richest lives don't happen by accident—the people living them are intentional about their calendar and thoughtful about what they engage in and what they don't engage in. Experiencing life is a cornerstone of what makes you, you. But what if you've spent your entire life focused on achieving and don't know how to "do" leisure? Or maybe you've been living someone else's version of experiences and adventure that doesn't fit you? It's time to hit your "reset" button.

In this chapter, you'll treat your life like one of those Choose Your Own Adventure books. First, you'll determine the optimal way you experience life, not just going through the motions because someone says leisure is good or prescribes it in a certain way. You'll examine your mindset to embrace that chosen version of experiencing life. You'll also learn practical ways to make this easier—because maybe you're great with others but don't necessarily thrive on your own. Or maybe it's the other way around. You'll discover and hone skills to be with others and also entertain yourself, whether it's taking an "awe walk" or designing a pilgrimage. Last, you'll engage and enrich your inner world, and revisit what's around you, beyond chasing new things.

SETTING INTENTIONS AND GOALS

To support your success in the exercises that follow, answer these questions about your intentions and goals for this chapter.

I want to feel _____ about the adventures and experiences in my life.

As I discover what matters through adventure or experiences, I want to become the type of person who _____

_____ .

This is what I want to accomplish from discovering what matters through adventure or experiences:

These are the mini-milestones I'm breaking this larger goal into:

_____ _____

_____ _____

_____ _____

_____ _____

_____ _____

_____ _____

_____ _____

_____ _____

_____ _____

_____ _____

_____ _____

_____ _____

_____ _____

_____ _____

_____ _____

DISCOVER YOUR OPTIMAL WAY TO EXPERIENCE LIFE

People sometimes forget to engage with the experiences life gifts them, instead running endlessly on the hamster wheel of obligations and work. Luckily, holidays allow you to engage more in the amazing things available to you. You may have a set blueprint for your holidays—a pattern you've unthinkingly adopted or consciously chosen. And then priorities change, and this blueprint doesn't fit into what matters to you now. This exercise helps you to design your optimal way of engaging with life's experiences.

Some people engage with experiences only on holidays, while others incorporate them in their everyday lives.

Where are you along this spectrum?

_____

_____

_____

_____

_____

When on vacation, some people are immersed in the experience. Others are lost in their head, overthinking or feeling dissatisfied.

Reflect on your personal vacation experiences overall:

_____

_____

_____

_____

_____

What's your general pattern of experiencing life?

Is it local, regional, or global? What forms of transportation do you prefer? What activities do you normally go for—more passive or active ones? Solo activities, or experiences that include others?

_____

_____

_____

_____

What else enhances the experience?

(e.g., getting dressed up, eating good food)

_____

_____

_____

_____

_____

Based on these reflections, what sort of experiences would you like to have more of?

_____

_____

_____

_____

What worries you the most about an experience?

(e.g., making others happy, budgeting, or the unfamiliarity)

_____

_____

_____

_____

What would be most realistic regarding experiences and adventures, considering your current life situation?

_____

_____

_____

_____

Understanding Why This Matters

Engaging with life's experiences, whether through an active adventure or noticing and then reveling in something in your daily life, should not be reserved for the rare vacation. Being fully in the moment of a great experience is a skill you need to practice regularly to cultivate openness, have more fun, and see the world through different eyes.

Connecting with What Matters

Here's what I've learned about
my relationship with engaging
with life's experiences:

_____

_____

_____

_____

_____

_____

Going forward, here's what
I'd like to do differently:

_____

_____

_____

_____

_____

_____

Taking Action on What Matters

Try these suggestions, then use the space here to reflect on how things went.

- Think about the experience enhancers you listed earlier, and how you might incorporate them into your next experience.
- Consider what you can do to mitigate the worries you've identified— do you have to work on practical actions or your mindset?
- Use the Rediscover Your Inner and Outer Worlds exercise later in this chapter to help you reflect.
- If you overplan or underplan, or the people you're with have different planning needs, see the Enjoy a Structured Ease to Exploring exercise later in this chapter.
- What are the three places or experiences you could discover within the next ninety days? Schedule them, plan them, and do them.

_____

_____

_____

_____

DESIGN YOUR MINDSET TO EMBRACE LEISURE

It can be hard to engage in leisure, but studies show that you need two to five hours of leisure every day for optimum functioning. The problem is, most people don't know what to do during free time, or believe they have to be productive all the time, especially the achievement-oriented or those clawing their way out of a crisis. These challenges start with your mindset around leisure, which you will explore in this exercise.

First, consider what you associate the word "leisure" with:

_____

_____

Read through the following statements and check the "Yes" box for the ones you agree with, and the "No" box for those you disagree with:

I think leisure is generally a waste of time.
☐ Yes
☐ No

I do not allow myself to have leisure time on weekdays.
☐ Yes
☐ No

I do not allow myself to have leisure time on weekends.
☐ Yes
☐ No

I do not allow myself to have leisure time when I have days off from work.
☐ Yes
☐ No

I do not allow myself to have leisure time when I'm on vacation.
☐ Yes
☐ No

I do not allow myself to have leisure time when it's a holiday.
☐ Yes
☐ No

I only engage in productive forms of leisure. (e.g., exercising, practicing a skill)
☐ Yes
☐ No

I see nonproductive forms of leisure as a waste of time. (e.g., hanging out with friends, sitting on a beach, watching TV)
☐ Yes
☐ No

If you answered no to at least three statements, then you find it hard to engage in leisure.

198 This Is What Matters

Understanding Why This Matters

We have only just begun to respect sleep as a cornerstone of life—the next step is to recognize leisure as an equally important fundamental. The pause during a break helps you to strategize and respond wisely to different situations instead of reacting. It gives you time to nurture your most important relationships, your body, and your curiosity. Having more experiences also means you have more raw material to help you come up with creative solutions or innovations.

Connecting with What Matters

Here's my greatest resistance toward leisure:

_____

_____

_____

_____

Here's what drives me toward leisure:

_____

_____

_____

_____

Taking Action on What Matters

People worry about what might happen when they engage in leisure activities. For instance, some believe that their careers or organizations might fall apart if they take a quick walk in the middle of the day or don't check in during a vacation. If this applies to you, ask yourself, "What's the worst that could happen if I did [activity]?"—and answer honestly. How likely is it that these outcomes would really happen, and what is your proof for these possibilities?

You could also pair your leisure activities with specific goals and aims. For instance, some people run to clear their heads and get fitter.

ENJOY A STRUCTURED EASE
TO EXPLORING

Some people are all for having a bucket list when exploring places, and then they frantically tear through that list, ticking off each item. Others are staunch advocates of camp "Free and Easy," winging it without a plan. The truth is, either can be stressful. Bucket lists may be based on someone else's preferences, or what you think you "should" engage in. On the other hand, you run the risk of getting little out of the trip when you have zero plan.

Reflect on the following prompts to figure out your relationship with structured explorations and free-and-easy ones, and find a balance between the two.

When you have a list of things to do and places to visit, you feel:

_____

_____

_____

_____

_____

_____

When you have no plan, you feel:

_____

_____

_____

_____

_____

_____

In the space between "adhere strictly to a checklist" and "completely free and easy," here's what you prefer, and why:

_____

_____

_____

Before your next exploration, use an app like Google Maps to create a map. Research and digitally pin the places or activities that you (1) definitely want to cover, and (2) are curious about and may want to cover. The first category will be the non-negotiables. For the second, as you explore that area or activity, you may engage with it, depending on how you feel in that moment. One guide may be: "If I'm feeling tired or hungry, I'll pop into a café to consult my pins and decide what activities I'm still up for."

Understanding Why This Matters

This exercise helps you to build in flexibility and structure, both essential in life. You have some guidance and ideas, plumbing the wisdom of others' recommendations. And you also have the freedom to thoughtfully choose what matters to you, and to change your mind along the way. This can be especially useful when you travel with people who have different flexibility or structure needs. You can also use these strategies for smaller-scale experiences; for instance, with the pieces you want to see in an art exhibition.

Connecting with What Matters

Here's what I've learned from this exercise about my exploration style:

_____

_____

_____

_____

_____

_____

_____

_____

_____

_____

Here's how I'd like to experience exploring differently:

_____

_____

_____

_____

_____

_____

_____

_____

_____

_____

Taking Action on What Matters

After doing this exercise, use the following reflections to guide you on how you can tweak your plan for future explorations:

- How did you feel when you first read this exercise?
- When doing the exercise, what did you notice yourself prioritizing? These could be categories of activities or places.
- Did you find yourself being more or less frazzled?
- Did you notice any difference in your time, mindset, or energy levels?
- If relevant, how did this method impact your exploration partner?
- Would you do this exercise again, and why?
- If you answered yes to the previous question, what would you do differently the next time?

LIST YOUR PROGRESS WITH A JAR OF AWESOME

In the wake of a crisis, there will be times when you don't want to engage with life and the experiences it has to offer. A crisis chews up energy you could otherwise dedicate to savoring life. And you may have lost some of your mojo, which translates to feeling helpless or hopeless. Or maybe you feel anxious and wonder if you're wasting time pursuing experiences that don't relate to your crisis while you're in the middle of it. Maybe you question if you even deserve these experiences. These are normal reactions, but they paralyze you. Your world shrinks as a result. And so you'll need to build a new habit, one that opens up your world again.

The Jar of Awesome is a habit-building tool created by bestselling author Tim Ferriss; it will help you build momentum and stay committed as you reengage with life experiences after a crisis. You will write down all the things you've done, so you can track your progress and therefore feel proud of yourself.

While motivation can feel impossible to create, especially during or after a crisis, momentum is easy enough to generate for yourself. Watching yourself take step after step, courtesy of the Jar of Awesome, creates a sense of pride. This is rewarding in itself, and the more you practice, the easier it becomes.

Start by listing any task, hobby, project, experience, etc., you've started or are carrying on with. Then take a few minutes every day to reflect on any steps you've taken toward these things (spending five minutes reading or watching a video about it, practicing the skill, etc.). Add these reflections to your list. Also, reflect on any new experiences you engaged with that day and add those to the list.

It doesn't matter how small the task is or how easily someone else might do it. People often protest against putting small or simple things on their list. An example is assembling flat-packed shelves. It may take two hours longer than the instructions say. Or the shelves may look a bit wonky in the end. That's okay. The point is, you did it!

You can do the same for the experiences or adventures you've committed to, even though you may think *All I had to do was show up!* Many people never show up. Even fewer continue.

Understanding Why This Matters

When you make time to fill your Jar of Awesome, you create a pause in your life. This allows you time away from your ever-racing thoughts and helps you take stock of what's going on. You feel more in control, instead of feeling stressed as the days and months go by. This boosts your mental fitness because you start making decisions from a calmer and wiser space. In other words, you are spending a little time to buy exponentially more time and contentment in the future.

The jar also creates accountability, because you see how you've continued to commit to this new habit. Often, people feel dejected when they break away from a new habit. But the jar helps you to learn the concept of "committing to recommitting," so you keep trying rather than talking yourself out of it. It also trains you to honor the things you start and the things you continue to show up for; both are equally important.

In that way, the jar teaches you to become more thoughtful about how you live your life and about the decisions you make, encouraging you to focus on what truly matters.

Connecting with What Matters

Looking at my jar, this is how I feel about myself:

_____

_____

_____

_____

_____

_____

This is how I see myself differently because of the awesome things I've done:

_____

_____

_____

_____

_____

_____

Taking Action on What Matters

Ideally, you'll spend five minutes every night putting things into your Jar of Awesome. You can also schedule monthly and quarterly reviews to take stock of what's in your jar. This way, you can reflect on how you've been growing and how you'd like to refine your processes and goals.

Here are some reflective questions to guide you:

These are the experiences I enjoy:

_____

_____

_____

_____

These are the experiences I find the easiest to engage in:

_____

_____

_____

_____

I enjoy these because...

_____

_____

_____

These are easiest because...

_____

_____

_____

Here's what I'll continue to do:

_____

_____

_____

_____

It's very easy to get excited reading a book on building habits, healing yourself, or changing something about your life. But it's not as easy to start or continue implementing your plans. Continuing to fill your jar is something you should be very proud of yourself for.

REDISCOVER YOUR INNER AND OUTER WORLDS

Writer Marcel Proust famously said, "The real voyage of discovery consists, not in seeking new landscapes, but in having new eyes." Sometimes people repeat activities because knowing what will happen next is comforting. Nevertheless, you may be surprised by what you can discover about yourself and your world when you look at things through new eyes. Rediscovering something involves both engaging thoughtfully in the moment and reflecting after the experience, rather than simply going through the usual motions on autopilot.

The following are some things you can rediscover, divided into what's internal (or indoors) and what's external (or outdoors).

1. Internal
   - Television shows, films
   - Books, poetry
   - Your home
   - Old journals, conversation logs

2. External
   - Social rituals (e.g., holidays, spiritual)
   - What you do and where you go on holidays
   - Your favorite cafés, restaurants, or food items
   - Galleries, exhibitions, museums
   - The great outdoors
   - Your evening stroll route

Adopting the mindset of discovery and curiosity will help in your rediscovery. Slowing down your pace, if you're walking, will also help.

Here are some reflections you can engage in during your rediscovery:

   - When was the last time I did this?
   - How have I changed as a person since last doing this?
   - How did I experience this differently, this time?
   - What made rediscovery easy or difficult?

The *internal* things I'd like to rediscover:

_____

_____

_____

_____

_____

The *external* things I'd like to rediscover:

_____

_____

_____

_____

Understanding Why This Matters

Both the novel and the familiar are essential in your personal life and relationships. Something new provides excitement and inspires discovery, while the familiar gives you a sense of safety. Sometimes, people get desensitized to new things and need a bigger dose of the exotic. This can become financially impractical, and also can make daily life feel unbearably dull. Rediscovering old experiences with fresh eyes helps you reflect on how you've grown, enlivens your day-to-day life, and improves your attentional capacity.

Doing this exercise, here's what surprised me:

_____

_____

_____

_____

_____

_____

_____

_____

_____

_____

From this exercise, I've learned this about my relationship with the familiar:

_____

_____

_____

_____

From this exercise, I've learned this about my relationship with novelty:

_____

_____

_____

_____

Taking Action on What Matters

First, decide how much of each internal or external discovery you'd like to embark upon, and how often. Schedule them into your calendar and commit to this practice.

You may decide to rediscover something with someone else. Here, exchanging ideas on your experiences may teach you more about yourself and each other.

Rediscovery also cultivates a sense of gratitude. You may consider what you've learned to be grateful for, through this practice. Also note how you may find your attitude toward your daily life evolving, or how your powers of observation may have developed.

TAKE AN AWE WALK

The simple act of walking can improve your mood, while a sense of awe can enhance your health and happiness and take you away from the chatter in your head. So, what if you combined the two? People experience awe primarily through a sense of physical vastness or novelty. But what if you didn't have to wait to climb a mountain or watch an avalanche to feel awe? The fifteen-minute "awe walk," studied by neuropsychologist Virginia Sturm's team, allows you to turn an ordinary walk into one where you're delighted by everyday surprises and inspiration.

Use the following questions to structure your awe walk.

Would you like to do it alone or with others?

(e.g., with a friend or family member, or even with a group)

_____
_____
_____

What are your favorite senses to engage?

(e.g., a soothing or dramatic sight or echoes in an old cathedral)

_____
_____
_____

What do you already love looking out for, that gives you that sense of awe?

(e.g., the moon, the sunset, and/or the sunrise, beautiful music, certain scents or plants)

_____
_____
_____

When you encounter the awesome things that you've identified, what do you do to engage further?

(e.g., take photographs, sit and admire, research the location more)

_____
_____
_____

How does doing that activity make you more engaged?

(e.g., your camera lens may help you concentrate, or researching might engage your curiosity)

_____

_____

_____

_____

When you compare your mood or outlook before engaging in what gives you a sense of awe, and then after, do you feel any different?

_____

_____

_____

_____

Where can you take awe walks?

Places that require some planning:

- A mountain, a hill, or a restaurant in a skyscraper where you can watch the sunrise or sunset, or see panoramic views.
- Somewhere with clear views of the night sky.
- The shore of a water body.
- Looking up from a trail lined with tall trees or dense buildings, or looking around a large stadium.
- A museum, gallery, planetarium, or aquarium.
- A historic building, a theater, religious monument, or mansion.
- A zoo or botanical garden.
- A forest, jungle, or island.

Everyday places:

- A different route on your daily walk or run.
- A part of your city you've never explored before.
- A park in your neighborhood.
- A fireplace or hearth, a storm, snowfall.
- A place that feels like your kind of sensory buffet—a specialist supermarket, makeup store, bookstore.

Understanding Why This Matters

When you walk, you trigger tons of chemical actions in your brain that makes it fitter and healthier. Your brain also produces chemicals that act like fertilizers for the blood vessels carrying nutrients to it. Walking after meals also lowers blood sugar levels. Imagine what happens when you combine these benefits with consciously training yourself to feel that sense of awe that reduces stress and inflammation and increases good feelings.

Awe is about feeling like you're in the presence of something mysterious, undefinable, or larger and more consequential than yourself. It takes you out of your head, expanding your perspective and giving you a break from racing thoughts. When you observe and appreciate the tiny wonders around you, an otherwise ordinary walk where you're rushing or not engaged turns into time well spent. And the thing is, you can never run out of awe. Every day has its beauty. No two sunrises or sunsets are the same.

The more you train yourself to look out for awe-inspiring moments, the more your brain learns to filter out unnecessary information like distracting thoughts, so you take in more joy!

Connecting with What Matters

These places feel the most accessible to me for an awe walk, in terms of interest and logistics:

_____

_____

_____

_____

_____

Following this exercise, here's how I've started to see the potential in enjoying my everyday life differently:

_____

_____

_____

_____

_____

Taking Action on What Matters

These instructions for taking an awe walk are adapted from the Greater Good Science Center at the University of California, Berkeley:

1. Turn your phone off (or to airplane mode if you plan to take photos).
2. Start with the mindset that you're discovering things with fresh eyes, and that you'll allow yourself to be delighted and curious.
3. Anchor yourself with your breath: Inhale deeply through your nose for six counts, feeling your belly expand, then exhale through your nose for six counts, feeling your belly contract. Notice the air moving through you and hear your breath.
4. Feel your feet on the ground as you walk. Shift your awareness to take in what's around you—anything that feels unexpected, delightful, vast.
5. Inhale for six counts, and exhale for another six counts.
6. Allow yourself to explore what inspires awe in you, moving from the vast to the small, and vice versa. It could be the scale of what's around you, the animals you see, or patterns of light and shadow.
7. Every so often, inhale and exhale again for six counts each. As you anchor yourself, notice everything around you that you'd otherwise miss. Immerse yourself in your different senses, and note what you enjoy the most.

EMBARK ON YOUR OWN
EVERYDAY PILGRIMAGE

Religion usually comes to mind when people think of pilgrimages. A pilgrimage is a special journey you undertake, often across different sites, where there's devotion and discovery. You can apply the same mindset to your everyday life. Each sight, sound, and experience can teach you something—if you give it the same respect and thoughtfulness that people give to religious pilgrimages. In this exercise, you'll design your own pilgrimages, based on the senses and themes you love or are curious about.

Consider activities and subjects you've always loved.

These may be things you catch up on during your free time, or when you tumble down that metaphorical rabbit hole online.

_____

_____

_____

Based on the following senses, jot down ideas of pilgrimages you're curious about.

Taste:

_____

_____

_____

Sight:

_____

_____

_____

Sound:

_____

_____

_____

Touch:

_____

_____

_____

Smell:

_____

_____

_____

Based on the following themes, jot down ideas of pilgrimages you're curious about.

Geographical location:

_____

_____

_____

History/Culture:

_____

_____

_____

Nature:

_____

_____

_____

Season:

_____

_____

_____

Others:

_____

_____

_____

The purpose of this exercise is to push the boundaries of your creativity. For instance, you could:

- Explore prosciutto-making, soy sauce factories, and salt shops under "Taste."
- Embark on a food pilgrimage of your city based on a culture (e.g., Middle Eastern food) or dish (e.g., almond croissants).
- DIY a route based on scenes in a book or film (e.g., the sites of *Angels & Demons* if you're in Rome).

How else can you explore?

Consider how you can combine this pilgrimage with other activities and goals, such as walking, strengthening relationships, and learning.

_____

_____

_____

_____

Understanding Why This Matters

Planning around a theme is an excellent way to focus your attention, look outside yourself, and engage with life creatively. The human brain likes to be efficient, so organizing things into categories helps it remember better. When you embark on your thematic pilgrimages, whatever you learn, reflect on, and experience can reinforce each other, so the activity makes a deeper impression. It's like studying your favorite subject or honing the skills of your sport—except *you* set the curriculum.

Connecting with What Matters

On a scale of 1–10, this is how excited I am about the pilgrimages I've identified, and why: (circle one of the following numbers)

1 2 3 4 5 6 7 8 9 10

_____

_____

_____

_____

Here's how things would be different during a pilgrimage from how I normally live:

_____

_____

_____

_____

Taking Action on What Matters

You may decide to invite some people to join you, so make the suggestion to those people with a few dates and times. Or put a call out on social media. If you're documenting the journey, consider what would be the easiest way to do that and even share what you document.

Some reflective questions for your pilgrimage:

- What did you notice about your headspace when pilgrimaging?
- What was your initial resistance, if any?
- What was the most enriching aspect of the pilgrimage?
- What did you enjoy the most?
- What surprised you the most?
- How would you tweak this experience for next time?
- How could you make the process easier next time?

DO SOMETHING, GROW YOURSELF

People often put off learning something unless it's for work, thinking they should wait until the perfect time. But sometimes the best time is now. This exercise invites you to consider what you can start to do or learn that will help create the best conditions for cultivating a life filled with what matters to you. You'll also figure out what might stand in the way so you can get going.

Some people are great with their hands, others with words. **Make a list of the things you're naturally good at:**

_____

_____

_____

Based on what you've identified, **is there any skill you'd like to develop further, or a new one you'd like to pick up?**

_____

_____

There are things that may be out of your comfort zone that you've always been curious about. **What are they?**

_____

_____

_____

As you look at the options you've identified, **come up with everyday and more "big treat" versions of each.**

For instance, an everyday version could be "take a two-hour scent-blending class in my city" and the big treat version could be "do a six-month course in Grasse."

_____

_____

_____

What are the biggest factors that stop you from pursuing these things? These challenges could be mindsets or practical considerations:

_____

_____

_____

What would make you most likely to do these things?

Some people might be open to doing a "big treat" thing with friends to share the experience and costs. Or maybe you'd like to experiment with the everyday version before committing to the big treat.

_____

_____

_____

Understanding Why This Matters

It's easy to say you don't know what to do, or that you just have some rough idea. When things feel abstract, you're more likely to put them off. By breaking things down according to what you're already gifted at and the other parts of you that you'd like to develop, and giving yourself a range of options for each, you inspire yourself into action.

Connecting with What Matters

Here's how I've realized I might
have been holding myself back:

_____

_____

_____

_____

_____

Here's what I've learned about
my options for doing things and
engaging more with life:

_____

_____

_____

_____

_____

Taking Action on What Matters

First, create an action plan for starting these activities. Write about where
you'd like to do something.

_____

_____

_____

_____

_____

Then enroll or get the necessary materials. If you are worried about how
you'll perform or feel anxious about other parts of your life, use the Reset Your
Brain exercise in Chapter 2 to ground yourself, and then consciously choose
to learn more about these activities you've identified.

You'll learn there are things you're great at and things you're not so
great at. Instead of feeling disheartened when you stumble, take these dis-
coveries as feedback, and keep rewarding yourself for choosing to show up.

RITUALIZING SUCCESS

You maximize success by getting clear on the journey, which is what you'll do in this exercise. First, you'll identify rewards, so your brain gets that feel-good dopamine boost whenever you do what you set out to do. Next, you'll figure out what stands in your way, so you're not surprised, but rather prepared to tackle these obstacles head-on. Then, you'll set mini-milestones so you can check in with yourself to ensure you're on track and practicing your new skills and habits without needlessly second-guessing yourself.

Rewarding Myself

I'll reward myself when I reach these mini-milestones:

_____

_____

_____

_____

Here's how I'll reward myself: (include both small and big rewards)

_____

_____

_____

_____

Identifying Obstacles

These are the factors that might make this journey more difficult:

_____

_____

_____

_____

Here's what I can do to get around these challenges:

_____

_____

_____

_____

These are the beliefs that stand in my way:

_____

_____

_____

_____

_____

Here's what I can do to get around these beliefs:

_____

_____

_____

_____

_____

Checking In

Here's how long I'll dedicate to discovering what matters to me right now: _____

I will check in with myself every _____ .

Putting It All Together

Now that you've filled out the previous sections, integrate them here. Then, set these review dates in your calendar:

Date:	Goal:
Date:	Milestone:
Date:	Milestone:
Date:	Milestone:
Where I am now:	

CONCLUSION: GOING FORWARD

"The sculpture is already complete within the
marble block before I start my work. It is already there;
I just have to chisel away the superfluous material."

—Michelangelo

As you think about who you've grown into as you've partnered with reality and worked through the exercises in this book, take a moment to consider:

- What did the idea of working through change feel like?
- Who were you at the beginning of the crisis?
- How have you evolved?
- Who are you now?
- What are you proudest of?
- What's surprised you the most about the journey, or yourself?
- What was your turning point?
- How does change feel to you now?

Consider, too, what did giving yourself this space to reflect on these questions teach you about change and your priorities?

When I "graduate" my clients from our work together, I invite them to imagine a parallel universe. One where life spins forward based on no active changes having been made. And I also invite them to consider what their life looks like right now, in the universe they are in. They break into smiles as they realize how these universes have diverged through the actions they have chosen to take.

Every step you take today can bring you either closer to or further from your different possible futures and the person you could become. And as that happens, your priorities will change. More life-changing events—some good, some bad—will inevitably come your way, *especially* if you live your life fully. After all, it's part of the human condition to experience life's ups and downs. And one of the hallmarks of emotional maturity is to know that you may change your mind and path, based on who you've become over time.

This book is here for you as your life changes. As you move forward, you may realize that stormier times become less threatening or shorter. Because you've learned to take care of yourself through the discomfort, you are able to thoughtfully choose what's wise for your emotions and your practical future. Through peaceful, stable times, you can experiment with life and engage with what it has to offer. Perhaps it's trying a lifestyle or mindset based on a suggestion someone else makes, and then reflecting on whether it's what you want. And then in times of celebration, you decide where you'd like to go from there. In other words, in the fact of life that you know as change, it's healthy to constantly reevaluate and realign, taking on what matters and discarding what doesn't. Whether in discomfort, experimenting with something new, or contemplating where you'd like to go, revisiting the exercises in this book can support you in the experience. Reflecting during these different chapters of your life will take you closer to the heart of who you are, much like Michelangelo's sculptures.

Changes are raw material for growth. They are the ways *through* life, because of what they reveal. May you allow crises, celebrations, and stability to be your teachers.

ABOUT THE AUTHOR

Dr. Perpetua Neo coaches Type A++ people with demanding lives to be in control of their heads, time, and relationships, so they perform and lead at their best always. She blends cutting-edge neuroscience, psychology, and ancient wisdom into plain English—to engineer lasting systems tailored to her clients' personalities, lifestyles, and goals—creating change quickly and deeply. Dr. P's specialty topics are sustainable high performance without burning out, exiting and building a meaningful, peaceful life after complicated domestic violence relationships, and leveraging the diverse ways in which people are wired. She was educated at the University of Cambridge and University College London, and her work has been published in *Forbes*, *Business Insider*, *Vogue*, *HuffPost*, and *mindbodygreen*, across forty-one languages. She has lectured for and spoken at London Business School, London's Institute of Directors, and London College of Fashion, and partnered with Lancôme to create a personality test to help people live their strengths. She consults for neurodiversity at Stanford University and was recognized as one of *mindbodygreen*'s twenty cutting-edge mental health leaders in 2020. Dr. P works in English and Mandarin-Chinese across six continents. She flies globally, or works via FaceTime or Skype, for one-on-one consultations, workshops, and speaking gigs. Learn more at PerpetuaNeo.com.